MW00815077

The Existence and Majesty of God

Stuart Greaves

Forerunner Books
Kansas City, Missouri

The Existence and Majesty of God
By Stuart Greaves

Forerunner School of Ministry
International House of Prayer

Published by Forerunner Books
International House of Prayer
3535 East Red Bridge Road
Kansas City, Missouri 64137
(816) 763-0200 Ext. 2675
forerunnerbooks@ihop.org
www.IHOP.org

Copyright © 2008 by Forerunner Books
All rights reserved.

This book or parts of this book may not be reproduced in any form, stored in a retrieval system, or transmitted in any form by any means—electronic, mechanical, photocopy, recording, or otherwis—without prior written permission of the publisher, except as provided by United States of America copyright law.

ISBN: 978-0-9798807-7-3

Unless otherwise noted, all Scripture quotations are from the New King James Version of the Bible. Copyright © 1988 by Broadman and Holman Publishers, Nashville, Tennessee.

Cover design by IHOP-KC Marketing
Interior design by Dale Jimmo

Printed in the United States of America

Table of Contents

Introduction

I. BEGINNING WITH THE KNOWLEDGE OF GOD

A. Abraham was the first person to catch the vision that God's plan and desire was to unite the physical and spiritual realms (Ephesians 1:9–10). Rabbi Zalman Baruch Melamed said:

> ***Avraham Avinu***, *our father Abraham, was the first person to successfully unite the physical and spiritual. Abraham sees as his central mission in life the elevation of existence from one level to the next, while maintaining full ties with [natural life]. From the moment that he discovers that there is one Creator who created one harmonious world, in which there exists no contradiction between body and soul, he tries to pass on this message to others in any way possible.*

B. *With this he begins the difficult process of* **Tikkun Olam** *(the mending of the world), setting his sights on his ultimate goal: the day when "God will be one, and His name one" (Zechariah 14:9). In order to bring about the complete union between the physical existence and the Creator, one must live in the Land of Israel. Israel, by her very nature, is an expression of the sanctification of the physical: a physical land, which is, at the same time, holy.*

C. *Accordingly, Abraham receives the commandment,* **"Lekh Lekha"**— *"Go away from your land, from your birthplace and from your father's house to the land that I will show you."[1]*

D. The Old Testament saints understood the revelation of the union of Heaven and Earth. Melamed declares:

    1. Abraham was the first person to have this insight into God's plan to reconcile Heaven and Earth.

    2. Abraham's ministry was to pattern to the nation that would come from him and the nations of the earth the value and truth of this reality.

---

[1] Melamed, Rabbi Zalman. "Parshat Lekh Lekha: Understanding Abraham." *The Beit-El Yeshiva Center.* http://www.yeshiva.org.il/midrash/shiur.asp?id=318.

*...having made known to us the **mystery of His will, according to His good pleasure which He purposed in Himself,** that in the dispensation of the fullness of the times He might gather together in one all things in Christ, both which are in heaven and which are on earth—in Him. (Ephesians 1:9–10, emphasis added)*

E.   God's premier vision is for the earth to be filled with the knowledge of His glory. The centerpiece of God's eternal purpose is for Jesus to come back to fully establish His Kingdom-rule over all the earth as He joins the heavenly and earthly realms together. Both heavenly and earthly dimensions must come together to fully express God's personality and purposes.

F.   God has designed the natural and the spirit realm to function in union with one another in order for both realms to enter into their full expressions.

G.   The joining of the realm of Heaven and the realm of the earth is for the purpose of filling the earth with the knowledge of God's attributes—the glory of His existence, personality, and purpose. The whole earth will be filled with this reality.

H.   Understanding the mystery of His will is essential to understanding God's plan of redemption.

Christian eschatology must be broadened out into cosmic eschatology, for otherwise it becomes a Gnostic doctrine of redemption, and is bound to teach, no longer the redemption of the world but a redemption from the world, no longer the redemption of the body but a deliverance of the soul from the body. But men and women are not aspirants for angelic status, whose home is in heaven and who feel that on this earth they are in exile. They are creatures of flesh and blood. Their eschatological future is a human and earthly future—the resurrection of the dead and the life of the world to come. According to the Christian understanding, the Redeemer is no other than the Creator. He would contradict himself if he were not to redeem everything He has made. The God who created the universe will one day be 'all in all' (1 Cor. 15.28).[2]

---

2   Moltmann, Jurgen. *The Coming of God* (Minneapolis: First Fortress Press, 1996), p. 259.

I.   The mystery of God's will is for Jesus to come back and unite the realm of the spirit and the realm of the natural. Chapter 17 of John's gospel focuses on the subject of how the central mission of Jesus' life and ministry was to reveal God's name and personality. This mission was what motivated Christ to go to the Cross. The Cross was the inauguration of a new revelation of God (Hebrews 1:1–2). When Jesus returns, He will continue that central mission of making the fullness of God's glory known in the earth forever.

II.   **JOURNEY TO THE VISION OF FULLNESS—GOD POSSESSES HEAVEN AND EARTH**

*Then Melchizedek king of Salem brought out bread and wine; he was the priest of God Most High. And he blessed him and said: "Blessed be Abram of **God Most High, Possessor of heaven and earth** (Abram gets the revelation); and blessed be God Most High, who has delivered your enemies into your hand." And he gave him a tithe of all. Now the king of Sodom said to Abram, "Give me the persons, and take the goods for yourself." But Abram said to the king of Sodom, **"I have raised my hand to the LORD, God Most High, the Possessor of heaven and earth** (Abram uses the new revelation of God), that I will take nothing, from a thread to a sandal strap, and that I will not take anything that is yours, lest you should say, 'I have made Abram rich . . .'" (Genesis 14:18–23, emphasis and parenthetical comments added)*

A.   The high priest, Melchizedek, brought the revelation of God as LORD, possessor of Heaven and Earth. I believe that this ushered Abraham into the vision for fullness and into the Genesis 15:1 encounter with the God of fullness. Genesis 15:1 is where humanity, through Abraham, is promised the fullness of God, which is fulfilled in his Seed—Christ.
*Now the LORD had said to Abram: "Get out of your country, from your family and from your father's house, to a land that I will show you. **I will make you a great nation; I will bless you and make your name great; and you shall be a blessing.** I will bless those who bless you, and I will curse him who curses you; and **in you all the families of the earth shall be blessed."** (Genesis 12:1–3, emphasis added)*

For the promise that he would be the heir of the world was not to Abraham or to his seed through the law, but through the righteousness of faith. (Romans 4:13)

B.   God extended a prophetic invitation to Abraham (Romans 4:13). However, from Genesis 12:1–3 to his visitation in Genesis 15:1, Abraham was faced with interesting circumstances. In them, though, he responded in faith, seeming to understand that the promise is to be secondary to actually desiring and pursuing God.

1.   Abraham sought God (12:7–8, 13:1–4, 13:18).

2.   The Promise Land was rightfully his, but he walked away from it, leaning into the sovereignty of God (13:8–9).

3.   God reassured Abraham of the divine promise (13:14–17).

4.   Abraham went to battle to rescue Lot and brought him back (14:14–17).

C.   After the war, Abraham was presented with another test when two kings came to him and made him an offer.

1.   Melchizedek offered Abraham a betrothal, a marriage or an engagement to God, which he accepted, making an oath to God (14:22).

2.   God entered into a covenant with Abraham that was likened to a marriage covenant (Genesis 15). In Genesis14:18, Abraham already belonged to God, but here God declared that He belonged to Abraham as well. In this covenant, He declared to Abraham that He would one day bring His people out of prison to make a covenant with the whole people (Exodus 19:5).

3.   The King of Sodom offered Abraham wealth, which he refused in light of his betrothal to God (14:21–24).

4.   The covenant in which Abraham belongs to God and God to Abraham (the Abrahamic covenant) is the basis of the covenant formula.

D.   The covenant formula: **I will be your God, and you will be My people.**
This promise will be realized when the reconciliation of Heaven and
Earth is fully manifested at end of the millennial kingdom. God intends
for His covenants to be experienced within the context of intimate
relationship with His people.

*After these things the word of the L*ORD *came to Abram in a vision,
saying, "Do not be afraid, Abram.* **I am your shield, your exceedingly
great reward."** *(Genesis 15:1, emphasis added)*

I will set My tabernacle among you, and My soul shall not abhor you.
I will walk among you and be your God, and you shall be My people.
(Leviticus 26:11–12, emphasis added)

*Then I will give them a heart to know Me, that I am the L*ORD*; and* **they
shall be My people, and I will be their God, for they shall return to Me
with their whole heart.** *(Jeremiah 24:7, emphasis added)*

You shall be My people, and I will be your God. (Jeremiah 30:22)

*But this is the covenant that I will make with the house of Israel after
those days, says the L*ORD*: I will put My law in their minds, and write it
on their hearts; and* **I will be their God, and they shall be My people.**
(Jeremiah 31:33, emphasis added)

They shall be My people, and I will be their God; *then I will give them
one heart and one way, that they may fear Me forever, for the good
of them and their children after them. And I will make an everlasting
covenant with them, that I will not turn away from doing them good; but*
I will put My fear in their hearts so that they will not depart from Me.
*Yes, I will rejoice over them to do them good, and I will assuredly plant
them in this land, with all My heart and with all My soul. (Jeremiah
32:38–41, emphasis added)*

Now **I saw a new heaven and a new earth***, for the first heaven and the
first earth had passed away. Also there was no more sea. Then I, John,
saw the holy city, New Jerusalem, coming down out of heaven from God,
prepared as a bride adorned for her husband. And I heard a loud voice
from heaven saying,* **"Behold, the tabernacle of God is with men, and
He will dwell with them, and they shall be His people. God Himself
will be with them and be their God.** *And God will wipe away every tear
from their eyes; there shall be no more death, nor sorrow, nor crying.
There shall be no more pain, for the former things have passed away.
(Revelation 21:1–4, emphasis added)*

III.   THE LIGHT OF THE KNOWLEDGE OF THE GLORY OF GOD

A.   I refer to Genesis 1:1–3 as God's vision statement. It gives us insight into God's purposes in creating the world. Where it is recorded that God declared, "Let there be light," there is no mention of the source of the light. The sources of the natural light were not created until the fourth day. It is my opinion that the reason for this is that the light that shone forth on the first day was the light of the knowledge of God's glory.
The city had no need of the sun or of the moon to shine in it, for the glory of God illuminated it. The Lamb is its light. And the nations of those who are saved shall walk in its light, and the kings of the earth bring their glory and honor into it. (Revelation 21:23–24, emphasis added)

B.   I believe that God was making a statement by declaring that the purpose for all of created order was so that the world could be filled with the knowledge of God.

C.   The light that shone forth came from the second Person of the Trinity.
*For it is the **God who commanded light to shine** out of darkness, who **has shone in our hearts to give the light** of the knowledge of the glory of God **in the face of Jesus Christ.** (2 Corinthians 4:6, emphasis added)*

Throughout the Old Testament, the prophets declared God's desire and plan to fill the earth with the knowledge of His glory — the full expression of God's personality, way and purposes.
*In the beginning God created the heavens and the earth. The earth was without form, and void; and darkness was on the face of the deep. And the Spirit of God was hovering over the face of the waters. **Then God said, "Let there be light"; and there was light.** (Genesis 1:1–3, emphasis added)*

*For it is the **God who commanded light to shine out of darkness,** who has shone in our hearts to give **the light of the knowledge of the glory of God** in the face of Jesus Christ. (2 Corinthians 4:6, emphasis added)*

*. . . But truly, as I live, all **the earth shall be filled with the glory of the LORD.** (Numbers 14:21, emphasis added)*

*And blessed be His glorious name forever! And **let the whole earth be filled with His glory.** (Psalm 72:19, emphasis added)*

*And one cried to another and said: "Holy, holy, holy is the L*ORD* of hosts; **the whole earth is full of His glory!**" (Isaiah 6:3, emphasis added)*

*For **the earth will be filled with the knowledge of the glory of the L**O**RD**, as the waters cover the sea. (Habakkuk 2:14, emphasis added)*

E.   True preaching confronts Earth with Heaven, in that it is the proclamation of the knowledge of the only true God and His Christ. The Apostle Paul reveals that his preaching was to shatter false paradigms concerning the knowledge of God. This means that Paul's preaching directed his listeners to the heart and the revelation of who God is.
*For though we walk in the flesh, we do not war according to the flesh. For the weapons of our warfare are not carnal but mighty in God **for pulling down strongholds, casting down arguments and every high thing that exalts itself against the knowledge of God**, bringing every thought into captivity to the obedience of Christ, and being ready to punish all disobedience when your obedience is fulfilled. (2 Corinthians 10:3–6, emphasis added)*

F.   The knowledge of God is truly the central issue before the Church in this hour. Everything rises and falls on the revelation of the knowledge of God. It is vital that our hearts and minds be daily renewed by the knowledge of God. Our vision needs to be ever expanding to transcendent heights.
*Hear the word of the L*ORD*, you children of Israel, for the L*ORD* brings a charge against the inhabitants of the land: **"There is no truth or mercy or knowledge of God in the land."** (Hosea 4:1, emphasis added)*

***My people are destroyed for lack of knowledge.** Because you have rejected **knowledge**, I also will reject you from being priest for Me; because you have forgotten the law of your God, I also will forget your children. (Hosea 4:6, emphasis added)*

***Let us know, let us pursue the knowledge of the L**O**RD.** His going forth is established as the morning; He will come to us like the rain, like the latter and former rain to the earth. (Hosea 6:3, emphasis added)*

***For I desire** mercy and not sacrifice, and **the knowledge of God** more than burnt offerings. (Hosea 6:6, emphasis added)*

IV.   THE NECESSITY OF EXPANDING OUR VIEW OF GOD

A.   The Church has surrendered her once lofty concept of God and has substituted for it one so low, so ignoble, as to be utterly unworthy of thinking, worshiping men.[3]

*Oh, **magnify the LORD** with me, and let us exalt His name together. (Psalm 34:3, emphasis added)*

*Be still, and **know that I am God**; I will be exalted among the nations, **I will be exalted in the earth!** (Psalm 46:10, emphasis added)*

B.   It is crucial that we exalt our vision of God back to its biblical proportions, producing awe-inspiring worship and the fear of the Lord in the hearts of the people of God. As A.W. Tozer said, "What comes into our minds when we think about God is the most important thing about us."[4]

C.   There is great need for the proclamation of the knowledge of God. True prophetic preaching is saturated with the knowledge of God, which confronts vain imaginations and earthbound ideas about the uncreated God.
*For though we walk in the flesh, we do not war according to the flesh. For the weapons of our warfare are not carnal but mighty in God for **pulling down strongholds, casting down arguments and every high thing that exalts itself against the knowledge of God**, bringing every thought into captivity to the obedience of Christ . . . (2 Corinthians 10:3–5, emphasis added)*

D.   The way that we live is dynamically related to our view of God. Our view of ourselves, others and life in general is profoundly affected by our idea or view of God. It is absolutely vital that we live a life that is conducive to pursuing and cultivating a proper view of God. Our knowledge of God is the most influential thing in our lives because what we believe about God will determine how we live.

---

3   Tozer, A.W. *The Knowledge of the Holy* (San Francisco: HarperSanFrancisco, 1961), p. vii.
4   Ibid., p. 1.

E.   Tozer said, **"We tend by a secret law of the soul to move toward our mental image of God."**[5] For this reason, it is crucial that the revelation of the knowledge of God found in Christ Jesus be the premier focus and top priority of our lives. We must intensely pursue the knowledge of God and make it the foundation of our souls.

> *One thing I have desired of the L*ORD*, that will I seek: that I may dwell in the house of the L*ORD *all the days of my life, to behold the beauty of the L*ORD *(the knowledge of God), and to inquire in His temple. (Psalm 27:4, parenthetical comment added)*

F.   It is important to know that the knowledge of God is more than a concept. It is a reality to be encountered on a deep heart-level. The knowledge of God, though filled with many intellectual concepts, is a theology of the heart. The revealing of God to the heart is exhilarating and powerful.

G.   *All the problems of heaven and earth, though they were to confront us together and at once, would be nothing compared with the overwhelming problem of God. That He* is*; what He is* like*; and what we as moral being must* do *about Him. The man who comes to a right belief about God is relieved of ten thousand temporal problems, for he sees at once that these have to do with matters which at the most cannot concern him for very long; but even if the multiple burdens of time may be lifted from him, the one mighty single burden of eternity begins to press down upon him with a weight more crushing than all the woes of the world pile one upon another.[6]*

H.   The very nature of idolatry is rooted in erroneous ideas of God. Idolatry is not only the worship of statues, but it is also the creating of God in **our** image. The first and second commandments of the Ten Commandments confront the issue of idolatry in the human heart. Idolatry arouses the jealousy of God.

> ***You shall have no other gods before Me.*** *You shall not make for yourself a carved image—any likeness of anything that is in heaven above, or that is in the earth beneath, or that is in the water under the earth; you shall not bow down to them nor serve them.* ***For I, the L***ORD ***your God, am a jealous God****, visiting the iniquity of the fathers upon the children to the third and fourth generations of those who hate Me, but showing mercy to thousands, to those who love Me and keep My commandments. (Exodus 20:3–6, emphasis added)*

---

5   Tozer, A.W. *The Knowledge of the Holy* (San Francisco: HarperSanFrancisco, 1961), p. vii.
6   Ibid., p.5.

These things you have done, and I kept silent; **you thought that I was altogether like you;** *but I will rebuke you, and set them in order before your eyes. (Psalm 50:21, emphasis added)*

I.   A. W. Tozer has stated, "The essence of idolatry is the entertainment of thoughts about God that are unworthy of Him."[7]

J.   *The Holy Spirit beckons us to enjoy intimacy with God by enabling us to experience the deep things of God. The Spirit discerns the deep things of God's heart (His emotions), mind (His plans) and power (His works in creation, redemption, New Jerusalem, etc) that we might know or "experience" them. God opens His heart so we can experience active intimacy with Him.[8]*
     "Eye has not seen, nor ear heard, nor have entered into the heart of man the things which God has prepared for those who love Him." But God has revealed them to us through His Spirit. For the Spirit searches (discerns) *all things, yes, the* **deep things of God** *. . . Now we have received . . . the Spirit who is from God,* **that we might know** (experience) **the things that have been freely given to us by God.** *(1 Corinthians 2:9–12, emphasis and parenthetical comments added)*

K.   The essence of eternal life is coming to the knowledge of God. The main point of eternal life is that people would be enraptured in the knowledge of God.[9]

---

7   Tozer, A.W. *The Knowledge of the Holy* (San Francisco: HarperSanFrancisco, 1961), p. 3.
8   Bickle, Mike. 2006. "Exhilarated by the Knowledge of God." The International House of Prayer, http://www.ihop.org/Publisher/File.aspx?id=100000024.
9   Ibid.

L.   *What so high and noble a subject, what so fit for his meditations or thine, as the highest and noblest Being, and those transcendently glorious perfections wherewith he is clothed! A mere contemplation of the Divine excellencies may afford much pleasure to any man that loves to exercise his reason, and is addicted to speculation: but what incomparable sweetness, then, will holy souls find in viewing and considering those perfections now, which they are more fully to behold hereafter; and seeing what manner of God, how wise and powerful, how great, and good, and holy is he, in whom the covenant interests them, and in the enjoyment of whom their happiness consists! If rich men delight to sum up their vast revenues, to read over their rentals, look upon their hoards; if they bless themselves in their great wealth, or, to use the prophet's words (Jer. ix. 23), "glory in their riches," well may believers rejoice and glory in their "knowing the Lord" (ver. 24), and please themselves in seeing how rich they are in having an immensely full and all-sufficient God for their inheritance. Alas! how little do most men know of that Deity they profess to serve, and own, not as their Sovereign only, but their Portion.*[10]

10   Charnock, Stephen. *The Existence and Attributes of God, Volume One* (Grand Rapids: Baker Books, 2005), p. 19.

Session One: A Divine Attribute

I.   DIVINE ATTRIBUTES—GOD DESIRES TO MAKE HIMSELF KNOWN

   A.   God made all things for Himself that He might disclose all that He is to His people. This disclosure is called the knowledge of God. God does not posses the description of an attribute; He is that which the attribute describes. For example, God does not have love. God is love.

   B.   God desires to make Himself known to His people.

   The anger of the LORD *will not turn back **until He has executed and performed the thoughts of His heart.** In the latter days **you will understand it perfectly.*** *(Jeremiah 23:20, emphasis added)*

   *But as it is written: "Eye has not seen, nor ear heard, nor have entered into the heart of man the things which God has prepared for those who love Him." **But God has revealed them to us through His Spirit. For the Spirit searches all things, yes, the deep things of God.** For what man knows the things of a man except the spirit of the man which is in him? Even so no one knows the things of God except the Spirit of God. **Now we have received, not the spirit of the world, but the Spirit who is from God, that we might know the things that have been freely given to us by God.** These things we also speak, not in words which man's wisdom teaches but which the Holy Spirit teaches, comparing spiritual things with spiritual. But the natural man does not receive the things of the Spirit of God, for they are foolishness to him; nor can he know them, because they are spiritually discerned. But he who is spiritual judges all things, yet he himself is rightly judged by no one. For **"who has known the mind of the** LORD **that he may instruct Him?" But we have the mind of Christ.*** *(1 Corinthians 2:9–16, emphasis added)*

   Thus says the LORD*: "Let not the wise man glory in his wisdom, let not the mighty man glory in his might, nor let the rich man glory in his riches; **but let him who glories glory in this, that he understands and knows Me**, that I am the* LORD*, exercising lovingkindness, judgment, and righteousness in the earth. For in these I delight," says the* LORD*. (Jeremiah 9:23–24, emphasis added)*

To me, who am less than the least of all the saints, this grace was given, ***that I should preach among the Gentiles the unsearchable riches of Christ, and to make all see what is the fellowship of the mystery, which from the beginning of the ages has been hidden in God*** *who created all things through Jesus Christ; to the intent that now* ***the manifold wisdom of God might be made known by the church*** *to the principalities and powers in the heavenly places… (Ephesians 3:8–10, emphasis added)*

. . . May be able ***to comprehend with all the saints*** *what is the width and length and depth and height—***to know the love of Christ which passes knowledge***; that you may be filled with all the fullness of God. (Ephesians 3:18–19, emphasis added)*

. . . Which He made to abound toward us in all wisdom and prudence, ***having made known to us the mystery of His will,*** *according to His good pleasure which He purposed in Himself, that in the dispensation of the fullness of the times He might gather together in one all things in Christ, both which are in heaven and which are on earth—in Him. (Ephesians 1:8–10, emphasis added)*

. . . That the God of our Lord Jesus Christ, the Father of glory, ***may give to you the spirit of wisdom and revelation in the knowledge of Him,*** *the eyes of your understanding being enlightened;* ***that you may know*** *what is the hope of His calling, what are the riches of the glory of His inheritance in the saints, and what is the exceeding greatness of His power toward us who believe, according to the working of His mighty power which He worked in Christ when He raised Him from the dead and seated Him at His right hand in the heavenly places, far above all principality and power and might and dominion, and every name that is named, not only in this age but also in that which is to come. And He put all things under His feet, and gave Him to be head over all things to the church,* ***which is His body, the fullness of Him who fills all in all.*** *(Ephesians 1:17–23, emphasis added)*

*. . .***The mystery which has been hidden from ages and from generations, but now has been revealed to His saints.*** *To them* ***God willed to make known*** *what are the riches of the glory of this mystery among the Gentiles: which is Christ in you, the hope of glory. (Colossians 1:26–27, emphasis added)*

II.   WHAT IS A DIVINE ATTRIBUTE?

A.   What God discloses or reveals about Himself is an attribute. The attributes of God are not limited to the ones that are referenced in the Word of God. The infinitude of God insists that He must possess infinite attributes that will not be disclosed until the age to come when we see Him face to face.

B.   I believe that there are infinite attributes and that the ones we know are only the ones that God choose to make known to us on this side of eternity.

The secret things belong to the LORD our God, but those things which are revealed belong to us and to our children forever, that we may do all the words of this law. (Deuteronomy 29:29)

C.   A divine attribute makes known to us that which is true and lies within the character and nature of the uncreated God. It shows us what God looks like and feels like.

D.   *An attribute, as we can know it, is a mental concept, an intellectual response to God's self-revelation. It is an answer to a question, the reply God makes to our interrogation concerning Himself.*[1]

*And the LORD passed before him and proclaimed, "The LORD, the LORD God, **merciful** and **gracious, longsuffering, and abounding in goodness and truth, keeping mercy** for thousands, **forgiving iniquity and transgression and sin, by no means clearing the guilty**, visiting the iniquity of the fathers upon the children and the children's children to the third and the fourth generation." (Exodus 34:6–7, emphasis added)*

E.   A divine attribute is not a part of who God is; it is the whole of Him. He cannot be fragmented into parts. God is not a total sum of all of His attributes, but rather He simply **is**.

*Then Moses said to God, "Indeed, when I come to the children of Israel and say to them, 'The God of your fathers has sent me to you,' and they say to me, 'What is His **name**?' what shall I say to them?" And God said to Moses, "**I AM WHO I AM**." And He said, "Thus you shall say to the children of Israel, '**I AM** has sent me to you.'" (Exodus 3:13–14, emphasis added)*

---

1   Tozer, A.W. *The Knowledge of the Holy* (San Franscisco: HarperSanFrancisco, 1961), p. 13.

F.   *A man is the sum of his parts and his character the sum of the traits that compose it. These traits vary from man to man and may from time to time vary from themselves within the same man. Human character is not constant because the traits or qualities that constitute it are unstable . . . God exists in Himself and of Himself. His being He owes to no one. His substance is **indivisible**. He has no parts but is **single** in His **unitary** being.*[2]

G.   *The doctrine of the divine unity means not only that there is but one God; it means also that God is **simple**, **uncomplex**, one with Himself. The **harmony** of His being is the result not of a perfect **balance** of parts but of the **absence** of parts. Between His attributes no contradiction can exist. He need not suspend one to exercise another, for in Him all His attributes are one. All of God does all that God does; He does not divide Himself to perform a work, but works in the total unity of His being.*[3]

---

2   Ibid., p. 14–15. Emphasis added.
3   Ibid., p. 15. Emphasis added.

Session Two: Exhilarated by the Knowledge of God: Five Conditions (Proverbs 2:1–5)

I. **WE ARE CALLED TO LIVE EXHILARATED IN THE KNOWLEDGE OF GOD**

   A. *The Holy Spirit beckons us to enjoy intimacy with God by enabling us to experience the deep things of God. The Spirit discerns the deep things of God's heart (His emotions), mind (His plans) and power (His works in creation, redemption, New Jerusalem, etc.) that we might know or "experience" them. God opens His heart so we can experience active intimacy with Him.*[1]

   "Eye has not seen, nor ear heard, nor have entered into the heart of man the things which God has prepared for those who love Him." But God has revealed them to us through His Spirit. For the Spirit searches (discerns) *all things, yes, the **deep things of God** . . . Now we have received . . . the Spirit who is from God, **that we might know** (experience) **the things that have been freely given to us by God.** (1 Corinthians 2:9–12, emphasis and parenthetical comments added)*

   B. God opens His heart that we might experience active intimacy with the Lord. Mike Bickle states, "The essence of eternal life is coming to the knowledge of God. The main point of eternal life is that people would be enraptured by the knowledge of God."[2]

   C. As we give ourselves to the place of intimacy and prayer, the Holy Spirit will skillfully unfold to us the knowledge of God over days, weeks, years and decades. The Lord is a master craftsman in the way that He leads humanity into all truth.

   *This is **eternal life**, that they may **know** (experience) You, the only true **God**, and **Jesus Christ** whom You have sent. (John 17:3, emphasis and parenthetical comment added)*

   D. There is not a poet brilliant enough or an artist creative enough who can even begin to conceive and depict what the Godhead has in store for us: to rule and reign with Them in friendship and partnership, establishing the purposes of God throughout all of eternity.

---

1 Bickle, Mike. 2006. "Exhilarated by the Knowledge of God." The International House of Prayer, http://www.ihop.org/Publisher/File.aspx?id=100000024.

2 Ibid.

E.   **Our inheritance and destiny** in Christ is to go far beyond "superficial Christian religion" to experience intimacy with God's heart that energizes our heart with God's power (Ephesians 3:16–19). We have been called into dynamic relationship with the Godhead. The more we grow in the understanding that God is calling us into friendship, the more we realize that many other things lose their appeal. God desires to be our reward.

You are My friends if you do whatever I command you. No longer do I call you servants, for a servant does not know what his master is doing; but I have called you friends, for all things that I heard from My Father I have made known to you. (John 15:14–15)

After these things the word of the LORD came to Abram in a vision, saying, "Do not be afraid, Abram. **I am your shield, your exceedingly great reward."** *(Genesis 15:1, emphasis added)*

. . . That He would grant you . . . to be strengthened with might through His Spirit in the inner man . . . that you . . . may be able to **comprehend** *(experience) . . . the width, length, depth and height—to know (experience) the love (affections) of Christ which passes knowledge (if unaided by the Spirit); that you may be filled with all the fullness of God. (Ephesians 3:16–19, emphasis and parenthetical comments added)*

F.   The subject of the knowledge of God, though filled with many intellectual concepts, is first and foremost a theology of the heart. It is more than acquiring information. The knowledge of God is to be studied; but more than that, it is to be an avenue for encountering Christ. Humans were created that we might experience the depths of the Holy Trinity. Our glory and destiny in God is to be swallowed up in the Trinity forever.

And now, O Father, **glorify Me together** *with Yourself,* **with the glory which I had with You before the world was** *. . . And* **the glory which You gave Me I have given them,** *that they may be one just as We are one:* **I in them,** *and* **You in Me;** *that* **they may be made perfect in one,** *and that the world may know that You have sent Me, and* **have loved them as You have loved Me.** *(John 17:5,22–23, emphasis added)*

God is faithful, by whom **you were called into the fellowship of His Son,** *Jesus Christ our Lord. (1 Corinthians 1:9, emphasis added)*

. . . That which we have seen and heard we declare to you, that you also may have fellowship with us; and **truly our fellowship is with the Father and with His Son Jesus Christ.** *(1 John 1:3, emphasis added)*

*The grace of the Lord Jesus Christ, and the love of God, and **the fellowship of the Holy Spirit**, be with you all. (2 Corinthians 13:14, NASB, emphasis added)*

G.   God reveals God to the human spirit to awaken love in us.

*I will declare it (the Father's name), that the love with which You loved Me **may be in them**. (John 17:26, emphasis and parenthetical comment added)*

H.   It takes God's power to love God. There is nothing more pleasurable or exhilarating than loving God by the power of God. **Our desire for God is God's gift to us.** It is an expression of His desire for us. The knowledge of God empowers the First Commandment. When God's character is systematically unfolded, it awakens love in His people.

I.   Moses cried out to see God's glory or the deep things of God's heart (emotions).

*And [Moses] said, "Please, show me **Your glory**." Then He said, "I will make **all My goodness** pass before you, and I will proclaim the **name** of the LORD before you." (Exodus 33:18–19, emphasis added)*

*And the LORD passed before him and proclaimed, "The LORD, the LORD God, **merciful** and **gracious, longsuffering**, and **abounding in goodness** and **truth, keeping mercy** for thousands, **forgiving** iniquity and transgression and sin . . ." (Exodus 34:6–7, emphasis added)*

J.   There is an outpouring of revelation coming from the Godhead. In as much as we avail ourselves and open our hearts to the Lord and say to Him, "Here we are," our desire for God will increase, and so will the free gift of the revelation of the knowledge of Him.

II.   DISCOVERING THE HIDDEN MYSTERY OF THE KNOWLEDGE OF GOD

*However, **we speak wisdom among those who are mature**, yet not the wisdom of this age, nor of the rulers of this age, who are coming to nothing. But **we speak the wisdom of God in a mystery**, the hidden wisdom which God **ordained before the ages for our glory**…(1 Corinthians 2:6–7, emphasis added)*

A.   Paul states that he was declaring to the Corinthians the wisdom of God, which we can also call the knowledge of God. According to Paul, it was for our glory that God ordained the deep things of the knowledge of God before the ages. Instead of saying that it was for our glory, one could say that the hidden things were ordained before the ages for our enjoyment.

B.   There are things that were hidden in the heart of God before the foundations of the earth for our glory, which He longs to reveal to our hearts, things that will cause us to be exhilarated in love. When God reveals these hidden things, our hearts get fascinated.

To them God willed to make known what are the riches of the glory of this mystery among the Gentiles: which is Christ in you, the hope of glory. (Colossians 1:27, emphasis added)

. . . Until He has executed and performed the thoughts of His heart. In the latter days you will understand it perfectly. (Jeremiah 23:20, emphasis added)

C.   The hidden things of God, or the mystery of the knowledge of God, are not evasive but rather they are plainly found in the written Word of God. Paul uses the phrase "the mystery" often, especially in Ephesians and Colossians when he talks about the things that were hidden from the generations passed but now have been made known to the apostles and the prophets, who have made them known to all the saints.

D.   The hidden things are a mystery, but they are not incomprehensible in that it still takes God to reveal them to the human heart. I define the spirit of revelation as that which causes the Holy Scriptures to be made alive and dynamic to the human heart.

These things we also speak, not in words which man's wisdom teaches but which the Holy Spirit teaches, comparing spiritual things with spiritual. (1 Corinthians 2:13, emphasis added)

But I make known to you, brethren, that the gospel which was preached by me is not according to man. For I neither received it from man, nor was I taught it, but it came through the revelation of Jesus Christ. (Galatians 1:11–12, emphasis added)

> *But when **it pleased God**, who separated me from my mother's womb and called me through His grace, **to reveal His Son in me**, that I might preach Him among the Gentiles, **I did not immediately confer with flesh and blood** . . . (Galatians 1:15–16, emphasis added)*

E.　　When the spirit of revelation touches us, it causes our hearts to be tenderized. The spirit of revelation causes the Scripture, which is living and active, to no longer be static to the believer's heart. Rather, it becomes dynamic, causing us to feel the impact of it on our hearts. The mystery of God has been declared by the Son of God in the gospels and has been expounded on by the apostles in the Word of God.

> *For I determined not to know anything among you except Jesus Christ and Him crucified. (1 Corinthians 2:2)*

F.　　Christ, through the Holy Spirit, reveals the mystery concerning the knowledge of God hidden in God's heart, as Christ is the mystery revealed.

> *. . . To the knowledge of the mystery of God, both of the Father and of Christ, in whom are hidden all the treasures of wisdom and knowledge. (Colossians 2:2–3)*

> *And without controversy **great is the mystery of godliness: God was manifested in the flesh** . . . (1 Timothy 3:16, emphasis added)*

G.　　One discovers God through Christ, and Christ alone. The experience of the knowledge of God comes from knowing Christ alone, as no man can come to the Father except through him. The Spirit, through the person of Christ and the Word, has given us free access into the realm of the knowledge of God.

> *Now we have received, not the spirit of the world, but the Spirit who is from God, that we might know the things that have been freely given to us by God. (1 Corinthians 2:12)*

III.　MYSTERY—THE CENTRAL PURPOSE OF GOD'S PLAN (EPHESIANS 1:9–10)

A.　　God's premier vision is for the earth to be filled with the **knowledge of His glory.** The centerpiece of God's eternal purpose is for Jesus to come back to fully establish His Kingdom-rule over all the earth as He joins the **heavenly** and **earthly** realms together. Both the heavenly and earthly dimensions must come together to fully express God's personality and purposes.

B. The whole earth is to be filled with the knowledge of His existence, personality and purpose, also known as the **attributes** of God. God's attributes are the expression of who He is, the revealing of His personality; and the whole earth will be filled with this reality.

In the beginning God created the heavens and the earth. The earth was without form, and void; and darkness was on the face of the deep. And the Spirit of God was hovering over the face of the waters. ***Then God said, "Let there be light"; and there was light.*** *(Genesis 1:1–3, emphasis added)*

For it is the God who commanded light to shine out of darkness*, who has shone in our hearts to give **the light of the knowledge of the glory of God** in the face of Jesus Christ. (2 Corinthians 4:6, emphasis added)*

*. . . But truly, as I live, all **the earth shall be filled with the glory of the LORD…** (Numbers 14:21, emphasis added)*

*And blessed be His glorious name forever! And **let the whole earth be filled with His glory.** (Psalm 72:19, emphasis added)*

*And one cried to another and said: "Holy, holy, holy is the LORD of hosts; **the whole earth is full of His glory!"** (Isaiah 6:3, emphasis added)*

For the earth will be filled with the knowledge of the glory of the LORD, as the waters cover the sea. (Habakkuk 2:14)

IV. THE SOVEREIGNTY AND PLEASURE OF GOD IN THE MYSTERY

A. The mystery of God was devised according to God's pleasure.

1. He **wanted** this plan.

2. The plan brings great **delight** to Him.

3. When we touch this plan, it will fill us with **delight** and bind our hearts to Him in a deeper way.

B. God purposed the plan within Himself.

1. He is the sole **architect** of the plan.

2. He found no inspiration outside Himself for this plan.

3. He reigns supreme in overseeing the execution of this plan.

V. THE BIG PICTURE

*He Himself gave some to be apostles, some prophets, some evangelists, and some pastors and teachers, for the **equipping** of the saints . . . for the **edifying** of the body of Christ, **till** we **all** come to the unity of the faith and of **the knowledge of the Son of God** (intimacy), to a perfect man (maturity), to the measure of the stature of the fullness of Christ. (Ephesians 4:11–13, emphasis and parenthetical comments added)*

A. Apostles, prophets, etc. will equip the Church until three things occur in the Church: unity, intimacy (knowledge of God) and maturity.

B. The knowledge of the Son of God does not refer to the introductory knowledge of Jesus that we receive at salvation, but rather the deeper knowledge, which refers to intimacy with God. This is the ultimate place that God is bringing His Church. True apostolic ministry will bring people into a depth of understanding of the splendor and the majesty of Christ Jesus.

C. Paul was anointed to preach on the riches, or the beauty, of the knowledge of Jesus.

    *. . . This grace was given, that I should **preach** . . . the unsearchable **riches of Christ** . . . (Ephesians 3:8, emphasis added)*

D. We need thousands of messengers with this Ephesians 3:8 anointing to unfold the riches of the splendor of Jesus. They will be tenaciously focused on the knowledge of Jesus.

E. The central issue of spiritual warfare is the knowledge of God. The Church is powerful when we grow in the knowledge of God. Satan assaults the knowledge of God by blinding people's eyes to it (2 Corinthians 4:4). Lack of the knowledge of God is what constitutes strongholds.

    *. . . Whose minds the god of this age (Satan) has blinded . . . lest the **light of the gospel of the glory of Christ** . . . should shine on them. We do not preach ourselves, but Christ Jesus . . . For it is the God who commanded light to shine out of darkness, who has **shone in our hearts** to give the light of the **knowledge of the glory of God** in the face (person) of Jesus Christ. (2 Corinthians 4:4–6, emphasis and parenthetical comments added)*

    *. . . Grow in the grace and **knowledge** of our Lord and Savior Jesus Christ. (2 Peter 3:18, emphasis added)*

*Grace and peace be multiplied to you **in the knowledge of God** . . . as His divine power has given to us all things . . . **through the knowledge of Him** who called us by glory . . . (2 Peter 1:2–3, emphasis added)*

F.   Many do not realize that the knowledge of God is within their reach. This was one of Paul's primary prayers for the Church, that they would have a vision for gaining the knowledge of God.

*. . . The Father of glory, may give to you the spirit of wisdom and **revelation in the knowledge of Him,** the eyes of your **understanding being enlightened;** that you may **know** what is the **hope of His calling** (our destiny), what are the riches of the glory of **His inheritance** in the saints (who we are to God), and what is the exceeding greatness of **His power toward us** who believe, according to the working of His mighty power . . . (Ephesians 1:17–19, emphasis and parenthetical comments added)*

VI.   FIVE CONDITIONS FOR CULTIVATING THE KNOWLEDGE OF GOD

*If you receive My words, and treasure My commands within you, so that you incline your ear to wisdom, and apply your heart to understanding; yes, **if** you cry out for discernment, and lift up your voice for understanding, **if** you seek her as silver, and search for her as for hidden treasures; **then** you will understand the fear of the LORD, and find the **knowledge of God**. (Proverbs 2:1–5, emphasis added)*

A.   Receive God's words—obedience as the response to what we hear

B.   Treasure His commands—meditation on the Word

C.   Incline your ear to wisdom and apply your heart to understanding—cultivate a teachable spirit

D.   Cry out for discernment and lift up your voice for understanding—prayer

E.   Seek her as silver and search for her as for hidden treasures—refuse to be denied

VII. CONDITION NUMBER ONE: A COMMITMENT TO SEEK 100-FOLD OBEDIENCE

If you will receive My words . . . (Proverbs 2:1a)

A. The Holy Spirit is the only One who can reveal Jesus to us. If He is quenched and grieved (Ephesians 4:30; 1 Thessalonians 5:19), we will not receive His revelation of His dear friend, Jesus. We cannot offend the Spirit and still expect Him to make Jesus known to our hearts in a deep way. **Prayer is no substitute for the intention to obey God.**

B. Our spiritual immaturity is very different from purposely resisting the Holy Spirit and refusing to obey Him. Charles Finney, an anointed evangelist in the 1800s, preached a sermon titled: "One Sin Persisted in Is Fatal to the Soul." Are there areas of deliberate disobedience in your life? Deliberate sin blocks spiritual progress and hinders your walk with the Lord. Make a consistent resolution to confess and resist sinful areas. Realize that God looks more at the sincerity of your intentions to obey than at your actual attainment of spiritual maturity.

VIII. CONDITION NUMBER TWO: A LIFE OF MEDITATION ON THE WORD OF GOD

If you will . . . treasure My commands (the Word) *within you . . . (Proverbs 2:1b, parenthetical comment added)*

A. God's commands speak of God's Word. We treasure God's commandments as we fill our minds with His Word. We dialogue with Jesus as a Person, or we have conversation with Him (prayer), as we meditate much on the Scriptures. It is impossible to grow in intimacy with Jesus without regular meditation on the Scripture.

B. We use our time to fill our mind with the Word of God so that our emotions would be affected. Without this part of God's grace, we will **never** grow substantially. My use of time is one of the most serious issues in my life. When people ask me to do something during the time I have scheduled for prayer and meditation on the Word, I usually say, "No, I have an appointment." I view my time with God as a real appointment. I do not want to neglect Him nor keep Him waiting.

IX.   **CONDITION NUMBER THREE: A TEACHABLE SPIRIT (HAVING A HEART OPEN TO CORRECTION)**

If you . . . incline your ear to wisdom, and apply your heart to understanding . . . (Proverbs 2:1–2, emphasis added)

*But on this one will I look: on him who is poor and of a **contrite spirit** . . . (Isaiah 66:2, emphasis added)*

An inclined ear that applies the heart to learn instead of resisting wisdom speaks of a teachable and humble spirit. A teachable spirit in our approach to life is essential. We cannot have a stubborn spirit that is not teachable before God or man. Many people who are zealous for God lack a teachable, humble spirit. We easily pick up biases from those with whom we grew up. We can become rigid and hard-hearted, defending our pet doctrines. It is far better to remain pliable and teachable. The Lord can bring the humble into the understanding of any truth they are lacking.

X.   **CONDITION NUMBER FOUR: PERSEVERING PRAYER FOR THE KNOWLEDGE OF GOD**

Yes, if you cry out for discernment, and lift up your voice for understanding . . . (Proverbs 2:3)

***Ask**, and it will be given to you; **seek**, and you will find; **knock**, and it will be opened to you. For **everyone** who asks **receives**, and he who seeks **finds** and to him who knocks **it will be opened**. (Matthew 7:7–8, emphasis added)*

A. We must actually pray for revelation of God. One of Paul's primary prayers is for the spirit of wisdom and revelation in the knowledge of God (Ephesians 1:17).

XI.   **CONDITION NUMBER FIVE: EXTRAVAGANT SEARCHING FOR DIVINE TREASURES**

If you seek her as silver, and search for her as for hidden treasures ... (Proverbs 2:4)

*It is the glory of God to **conceal** a matter, but the glory of kings is to **search out** a matter. (Proverbs 25:2, emphasis added)*

A kingly spirit refuses to be denied. Extravagant searching for God includes a commitment to regular fasting. Fasting does not earn God's favor. Rather, it enlarges our capacity to freely receive from God as it leads to the tenderizing of our heart. If we can live without more of God, then we will go without more of God. We must be willing to spend long hours and pay any price in our quest to find the knowledge of God. We search for Him like a covetous man pursues wealth: with persistence and endurance. Many attend higher education for up to eight–ten years, laboring for wisdom to excel in their occupation. Perseverance is considered normal for any who seek to excel.

XII.   THE TWOFOLD DIVINE PROMISE

Then *you will understand the* ***fear of the LORD****, and find the* ***knowledge of God.*** *(Proverbs 2:5, emphasis added)*

The knowledge of God is the ultimate reality that the human spirit can experience in this age and in the age to come. The end-time Church will have a vision to go deep in the knowledge of God (Ephesians 4:13) and will intercede for the release of revelation (Ephesians 1:17) until receiving the anointing to make the riches of Jesus known to others (Ephesians 3:8).

Session Three: The Knowledge of God—The Mission of Christ Jesus, Part 1

I.   **THE KNOWLEDGE OF GOD: THE VISION OF THE CROSS (JOHN 17:1)**

    A.   John 17 is commonly known as the High Priestly prayer. The central theme of this great prophetic prayer is Jesus' zeal for the eternal purpose and knowledge of God. The Father will answer His Son's request, making this not only a prayer, but also a prophecy for the Church at the end of the age.

    B.   This prayer is probably the deepest and clearest expression of the heart of Christ as it is His fervent prayer before His passion and intercession at the cross of Calvary. This prayer contains the heartbeat (foundation) of Christ's intercession (Romans 8:26–27; 1 Corinthians 2:9–11; Hebrews 7:25; 1 John 2:1; Revelation 8:1–3).

    C.   I imagine the Father asking His Son, "Jesus, what can I give to You for dying on the cross?" Jesus' response is most overwhelming, "Father, I want them to know You!"

    Jesus spoke these words, lifted up His eyes to heaven, and said: "Father, the hour has come. Glorify Your Son, that Your Son also may glorify You . . ." (John 17:1)

    But they were hearing only, "He who formerly persecuted us now preaches the faith which he once tried to destroy." **And they glorified God in me.** *(Galatians 1:23–24, emphasis added)*

    D.   The culmination of Christ's ministry is in the Cross, where He accomplished the will of God forever, setting into motion God's eschatological plan. All that the Word of God declares in regard to eschatology flows out of the reality of the Cross. It is for this reason that Christ crucified, the Lamb of God, is the central figure of the book of Revelation. The Cross is what makes everything we see in the book of Revelation possible.

E.   God's purposes, plans, and power are made possible through and flow out of the reality of the Cross of Christ. When Christ declared, "It is finished!" it was more than a declaration of the fact that our sins can be forgiven, it also meant that now all things are ready for the fullness of God's purposes to be released and expressed from now on and forever.

F.   John 17 reveals the thunder of the Cross and the glory of the Passover Lamb of God. In this wondrous chapter, the glory of the Lamb is unveiled. We see here probably the clearest exposition of Christ's heart and the joy that was set before Him, which enabled Him to endure the Cross and despise its shame. This desire is also to become the mission of the apostolic Church throughout history, but in particular at the end of the age.

G.   The knowledge of God is the central issue of our personal spiritual experience in Christ, and it is the central issue of apostolic ministry to call the people of God to it as well.

H.   When the Lamb unfolds and administrates the judgments of the book of Revelation, what is beating in His heart is the longing declared in John 17: that the earth would be filled with the knowledge of the glory of the Lord like the waters cover the seas—the full expression of the knowledge of God in the earth.

        As You sent Me into the world, I also have sent them into the world. (John 17:18)

I.   The reality of the Cross will be the culmination of the Church at the end of the age. Out of the nations of the earth, the Father is fashioning a Bride who will be equally yoked to the Lamb of God. Christ will marry a Bride who was prepared in the way He was prepared, and that is through the reality of the Cross. It is for this reason that she is called the "Lamb's wife." This designation reflects the nature of which she is to partake and marry into—that of the Cross. It is the reality of knowing Him in the fellowship of His sufferings and the power of the resurrection.

J.   The way to glory is through death. Christ states here that His heart is ready to walk out that for which He came. Jesus came to serve and to give His life as a ransom for many. The Cross is the doorway into the glory of God.

K.   In John 12:27–29, the Father said that He glorified and would again glorify His name. The Father glorified His name by sending His Son to the cross to die. It was fitting for the Father that His Son would suffer in order to bring many to glory (Hebrews 2:10).

L.   The vastness of God's splendor is revealed in the Cross of Christ. Jesus' glory was first manifested at the wedding in Cana. The glory of Christ is significantly related to the Bridal Paradigm, in which we see Jesus as the heavenly Bridegroom. God's glory is the infinite width, length, depth and height of His love.

> *For even the **Son of Man** did not **come** to be served, but **to serve**, and **to give His life a ransom** for many. (Mark 10:45, emphasis added)*

> *"Now My soul is troubled, and what shall I say? 'Father, save Me from this hour'? **But for this purpose I came to this hour.** Father, glorify Your name." Then a voice came from heaven, saying, "I have both glorified it and will glorify it again." Therefore the people who stood by and heard it said that it had thundered. Others said, "An angel has spoken to Him." (John 12:27–29, emphasis added)*

> ***For it was fitting for Him** (the Father), for whom are all things and by whom are all things, in bringing many sons to glory, to make the **captain of their salvation** (Christ Jesus) perfect through sufferings. (Hebrews 2:10, emphasis and parenthetical comments added)*

II.   ALL AUTHORITY: CHRIST DISPENSES THE KNOWLEDGE OF GOD

> *. . . As You have given Him authority over all flesh, that He should give eternal life (the knowledge of God) to as many as You have given Him. (John 17:2, parenthetical comment added)*

A.   Christ suffered in obedience to the Father and thus He was given authority over all flesh. The Father has entrusted leadership over all humanity to Jesus. The earth and its fullness belong to YHWH, and He has given leadership of it to the Son of Man.

> *For in that **He** (the Father) **put all in subjection under him, He left nothing that is not put under him.** But now we do not yet see all things put under him. But we see Jesus, who was made a little lower than the angels, **for the suffering of death crowned with glory and honor,** that He, by the grace of God, **might taste death for everyone.** (Hebrews 2:8–9, emphasis and parenthetical comment added)*

B.   All authority in Heaven and on Earth has been given to Jesus, who is the pathway to the Father. Jesus has the authority to reveal the fullness of God and bring His people into it. The fullness of God speaks of experiencing the fullness of His power, heart, plans and purpose, that we might partner with Him and enjoy His embrace.

C.   Christ is the Forerunner who went beyond the veil into the Presence and secured a place for us. Jesus has the authority and the permission of the Father to bring humanity into the full experience of the knowledge of God. It is through Christ that we have access to the knowledge of God. This is not just a subject but a realm in the heart of God and an experiential reality.

> . . . *Where **the forerunner has entered for us, even Jesus**, having become High Priest forever according to the order of Melchizedek. (Hebrews 6:20, emphasis added)*

> *Forerunner: The writer to the Hebrews uses a most illuminating word about Jesus. He says that he entered the presence of God as our forerunner. The word is προδρομοσ. It has three stages of meaning. (i) It means one who rushes on. (ii) It means a pioneer. (iii) It means a scout who goes ahead to see that it is safe for the body of the troops to follow. Jesus went into the presence of God to make it safe for all men to follow.[1]*

> *The voice of one crying in the wilderness: "**Prepare the way of the LORD**; Make straight in the desert a highway for our God. Every valley shall be exalted And every mountain and hill brought low; The crooked places shall be made straight and the rough places smooth; **The glory of the LORD shall be revealed, and all flesh shall see it together**; For the mouth of the LORD has spoken." (Isaiah 40:3–5, emphasis added)*

D.   The consummation of all perfection is the Trinity invading the planet. Christ came and walked on the earth, died, and ascended into Heaven. The Holy Spirit now lives in His Church and has been preparing it for the last 2,000 years. The climax will be when the Spirit and the Church are in perfect unity, calling Jesus to return to the earth.

---

1   Barclay, William. *The Letter to the Hebrews*. The Daily Study Bible series, rev. ed. (The Westminster Press: Philadelphia, 2000, c. 1975), as quoted in *Scholar's Library: Silver* (Logos Bible Software: 2004). Emphasis added.

E.   Jesus will prepare the earth for 1,000 years for His Father to come and inhabit the planet. When Christ returns to the earth, it will be to prepare the planet to fully manifest that which has been accomplished on the Cross—the reconciliation of the realm of the spirit and the realm of the natural, and the glory of the Trinity covering the earth.

*And this is **eternal life**, that they may **know You, the only true God, and Jesus Christ** whom You have sent. (John 17:3, emphasis added)*

F.   Eternal life is entering into the experience of God and His Christ. Christ came to bring us into glory, that we might enter into the communion and fellowship of the Godhead forever. Eternal life, though it is ongoing, unending life, speaks **primarily** of the **quality** of life that one will live in eternity. Every human being will live forever, but not all will enter into the ecstatic reality of the knowledge of the glory of God in Christ. Eternal life is a quality of life that is experienced in the inner man in part now, but fully in the age to come. Christ says in John 14:1 to not have a troubled heart. He is essentially telling His disciples to enter in to eternal life (John 14:2, 17:3).

*Let not your heart be troubled; **you believe in God, believe also in Me**. In My Father's house are many mansions; if it were not so, I would have told you. I go to prepare a place for you. (John 14:1–2, emphasis added)*

*And this is eternal life, **that they may know You, the only true God, and Jesus Christ** whom You have sent. (John 17:3, emphasis added)*

G.   Eternal life is more than living forever, because every human being is going to live forever. It is a matter of what will be the quality of life humans will experience forever—the torment of damnation or the ecstasy of the knowledge of God. Born-again believers will experience the glory of the knowledge of God and intimacy with Him, which Christ calls eternal life. It is more the quality than the quantity of life.

H.   Christ prays that through Him humans might know the only true God. There are many false gods, but there is only one true God, and Christ is the only way to Him.

I.   **The issue of the true knowledge of God is and will continue to be crucial in this hour because of the increase of syncretism and religious mixture.** Jesus makes it very clear that there is only one God who alone is true. The essence of Jesus' prayer is that He would be glorified and the Father would be glorified through Him. God is glorified in many ways, but **the ultimate expression will be when the fullness of God's glory fills the earth.**

*. . . Having made known to us **the mystery of His will**, according to His good pleasure which He purposed in Himself, that in the dispensation of the fullness of the **times He might gather together in one all things in Christ, both which are in heaven and which are on earth—in Him.** (Ephesians 1:9–10, emphasis added)*

*After these things the word of the LORD came to Abram in a vision, saying, "Do not be afraid, Abram. **I am your shield, your exceedingly great reward.**" (Genesis 15:1, emphasis added)*

*Then the LORD said: "I have pardoned, according to your word; but truly, as I live, **all the earth shall be filled with the glory of the LORD . . .**" (Numbers 14:20–21, emphasis added)*

*And blessed be His glorious name forever! **And let the whole earth be filled with His glory.** (Psalm 72:19, emphasis added)*

*And one cried to another and said: "Holy, holy, holy is the LORD of hosts; **the whole earth is full of His glory!**" (Isaiah 6:3, emphasis added)*

*For **the earth will be filled** with the knowledge of the glory of the LORD, **as the waters cover the sea.** (Habakkuk 2:14, emphasis added)*

J.   The Man Christ Jesus is the only authorized dispenser and giver of the knowledge of God. God has spoken in these days in and through His Son. In John 17:26, Jesus declared to the Father that He (Jesus) will continue to declare the knowledge of God to His people. What is striking about this statement is that it is one of the last declarations Jesus makes before dying on the cross. Of all the promises He could have made to the Father, He promises that He would declare to humans the splendor of God forever. The very countenance of the Son of God reflects the Father's glory. To see Jesus is to see the Father (2 Corinthians 4:6). The Father has granted Jesus authority for the sole purpose of leading the human heart into the knowledge of God. True ministry in the Kingdom is fueled and driven by this mission.

*For it is the God who commanded light to shine out of darkness, who has shone in our hearts to **give the light of the knowledge of the glory of God in the face of Jesus Christ**. (2 Corinthians 4:6, emphasis added)*

*And I have declared to them **Your name**, and will declare it, that the love with which You loved Me may be in them, and I in them. (John 17:26, emphasis added)*

***God, who at various times and in various ways spoke** in time past to the fathers by the prophets, has in these **last days spoken to us by His Son**... (Hebrews 1:1–2, emphasis added)*

*And He Himself gave some to be apostles, some prophets, some evangelists, and some pastors and teachers, for the equipping of the saints for the work of ministry, for the edifying of the body of Christ, **till we all come to the unity of the faith and of the knowledge of the Son of God**, to **a perfect man**, to the measure of **the stature of the fullness of Christ**; that we should no longer be children, tossed to and fro and carried about with every wind of doctrine, by the trickery of men, in the cunning craftiness of deceitful plotting, but, **speaking the truth in love, may grow up in all things into Him who is the head—Christ—** from whom the whole body, joined and knit together by what every joint supplies, according to the effective working by which every part does its share, causes growth of the body for the edifying of itself in love. (Ephesians 4:11–16, emphasis added)*

*For both He who sanctifies and those who are being sanctified are all of one, for which reason He is not ashamed to call them brethren, saying: "**I will declare Your name to My brethren**; In the midst of the assembly I will sing praise to You." (Hebrews 2:11–12, emphasis added)*

III.   ETERNAL LIFE: TO BE SWALLOWED IN THE KNOWLEDGE OF THE GODHEAD FOREVER

And this is eternal life, that they may know You, the only true God, and Jesus Christ whom You have sent. (John 17:3)

A.   True life, true contentment or fulfillment, is only experienced in as much as our beings are filled with the knowledge of God. The knowledge of God is more than a subject. Rather, it is a realm of encountering and experiencing God. It is the reality of intimately knowing God.

B.   It is such a surprising concept that the uncreated God who has need of nothing desires and longs to be known by humans. The knowledge of God is the only way to find life and true rest for our souls.

*For this reason we also, since the day we heard it, **do not cease to pray for you**, and to ask that you may be **filled with the knowledge of His will** in all wisdom and spiritual understanding . . . (Colossians 1:9, emphasis added)*

C.   One of the definitive realities of death is unresponsiveness. Before Christ, we were dead in our sins; death was operating in our spirits, making it impossible for us to respond to the knowledge of God—the very source of life.

D.   The born-again experience makes us alive to God in Christ Jesus (Romans 6:11). Through Christ, we are now able to live because we can know, receive and respond to the knowledge of God. To live is to experience God. True life is to commune with God, to be satisfied and to have our spirits fed on the beauty and splendor of Almighty God. Christ is our life, and it is no wonder that He referred to Himself as Bread and Water, which are the basic necessities to live and survive. Christ is the sustainer of our hearts. In Psalm 73, the psalmist had it right when he said that God is the strength of our hearts and our portion forever.

My flesh and my heart fail; but God is the strength of my heart and my portion forever. (Psalm 73:26)

*Likewise you also, reckon yourselves to be dead indeed to sin, but **alive to God in Christ Jesus our Lord**. (Romans 6:11, emphasis added)*

*When **Christ who is our life** appears, then you also will appear with Him in glory. (Colossians 3:4, emphasis added)*

Session Four: The Knowledge of God–The Mission of Christ Jesus, Part 2

I. **OUR CAPTAIN, MADE PERFECT THROUGH SUFFERINGS, BRINGS US TO GLORY**

For it was fitting for Him, for whom are all things and by whom are all things, in bringing many sons to glory, to make the captain of their salvation perfect through sufferings. (Hebrews 2:10)

I have glorified You on the earth. I have finished the work (Hebrews 2:10) *which You have given Me to do. And now,* ***O Father, glorify Me together with Yourself****, with the glory which I had with You before the world was. (John 17:4–5, emphasis and parenthetical comment added)*

A. Through the sufferings of Christ, we are brought back into the Garden of God, which is the New Jerusalem, the place of communion, from which we have dominion over the earth under the leadership of the Son of God.

B. "For it was fitting for Him"—meaning, the passion of the Father. All things are for Him, made by Him, and it seems unthinkable that the uncreated God, who is infinite in His greatness, YHWH, would have the Second Person of the Trinity become a Man who would suffer. The writer of Hebrews declares that it was consistent with the Father's nature to do so; it was fitting for Him.

C. That which the Father did in Christ was in accordance with His divine nature and consistent with love.

   For God so loved the world that He gave His only begotten Son*, that whoever believes in Him should not perish but have everlasting life. (John 3:16, emphasis added)*

D. In Genesis 15:1, the Father established a solemn oath with Abraham that we would be the inheritors of His glory. The passion of the Godhead is to be the inheritance of the redeemed. God promised us the fullness of Himself.

After these things the word of the LORD came to Abram in a vision, saying, "Do not be afraid, Abram. I am your shield, your exceedingly great reward." (Genesis 15:1)

E.   Jesus is the pioneer of glory and the captain of our salvation; He came to lead us into glory.

    1.   The Greek word *archegos* means someone who starts something that others may enter into. It refers to someone who leaves an inheritance or legacy, or even a trailblazer.

    2.   One could use the illustration of a ship that has run upon rocks in shallow water. The *achegos* figure would be the one who swims to shore to secure the line before his shipmates follow.

*Let not your heart be troubled; you believe in God, believe also in Me. **In My Father's house are many mansions**; if it were not so, I would have told you. **I go to prepare a place for you. And if I go and prepare a place for you, I will come again and receive you to Myself**; that where I am, there you may be also. (John 14:1–3, emphasis added)*

II.   THE FATHER PREPARED A SACRIFICE SO THE REDEEMED COULD ENTER

For it was fitting for Him, for whom are all things and by whom are all things, in bringing many sons to glory, to make the captain of their salvation perfect through sufferings. (Hebrews 2:10)

A.   In the movie *The Passion of the Christ*, Jesus prayed, "Father, My heart is ready…"[1]

    1.   The pioneer was qualified through the things He suffered.

    2.   *Teleions* (Greek) is an unblemished animal fit for sacrifice.

    3.   He was made mature, equipped to fully carry out the purpose for which He came.

    4.   Christ had thirty-three years to prepare for the sacrifice of His passion.

---

1   *The Passion of the Christ,* DVD, directed by Mel Gibson (2004; Los Angeles, CA: Twentieth Century Fox, 2004).

*Therefore, **when He came into the world** (the first advent), He said: "Sacrifice and offering You did not desire, **but** a body You have prepared for Me. In burnt offerings and sacrifices for sin You had no pleasure. Then I said, 'Behold, I have come—**in the volume of the book it is written of Me** (in the book before the ages began)—to do Your will* (this was always in the plan and the heart of God . . . it was fitting for Him (Hebrews 2:10), *O God." Previously saying, "Sacrifice and offering, burnt offerings, and offerings for sin You did not desire, nor had pleasure in them" (which are offered according to the Law), then He said, "Behold, I have come to do Your will, O God." He takes away the first that He may establish the second. By that will we have been sanctified through the offering of the body of Jesus Christ once for all." (Hebrews 10:5–10, emphasis and parenthetical comments added)*

B.   The first advent of Christ was to offer His life as a ransom for many. Christ came to die and reveal the depths of the Father's love.

*For God so loved the world that **He** (the Father) **gave His only begotten Son**, that whoever believes in Him should not perish but have everlasting life. (John 3:16, emphasis and parenthetical comment added)*

*For even **the Son of Man** did not **come** to be served, but to serve, and **to give His life a ransom for many.** (Mark 10:45, emphasis added)*

*But God demonstrates His own love toward us, in that while we were still sinners, **Christ died for us.** (Romans 5:8, emphasis added)*

To Him who loved us and washed us from our sins in His own blood... *(Revelation 1:5, emphasis added)*

C.   Christ understood His mission and for what purpose He came to the earth (Psalm 40:6–8). He had a fundamental understanding that the Father was not after sacrifices, but that He was the Lamb of God to take away the sins of the world. In eternity past, the Second Person of the Trinity knew and understood that there was a human frame designed for Him to take on that would result in the perfect sacrifice.

*. . . In the Book of Life of the **Lamb slain from the foundation of the world.** (Revelation 13:8, emphasis added)*

D.   Christ came to carry out, once and for all, the sacrifice for the eternal plan of God. The mystery of the ages is that, through the Cross of Christ, God's eternal purpose prepared for our glory might be made manifest. The plan is that we would be in the glory of the Holiest of All forever.

*By that will we have been sanctified through the **offering of the body of Jesus Christ once for all.** (Hebrews 10:10, emphasis added)*

*However, we speak wisdom among those who are mature, yet not the wisdom of this age, nor of the rulers of this age, who are coming to nothing. But we speak the wisdom of God in a mystery, **the hidden wisdom which God ordained before the ages for our glory**, which none of the rulers of this age knew; for had they known, they would not have **crucified the Lord of glory.** (1 Corinthians 2:6–8, emphasis added)*

***And the glory which You gave Me I have given them**, that they may be one just as We are one . . . (John 17:22, emphasis added)*

E.   Christ was first to do away with the Old Covenant and carry out the eternal longing of God. Hebrews 9:9 tells us that Jesus said, **"Behold, I come to do Your will."** God provided the Lamb for Himself because He wanted a people sanctified for Him through a sacrifice prepared and offered by Him.

*For **of** Him and **through** Him and **to** Him **are all things**, to whom be glory forever. Amen. (Romans 11:36, emphasis added)*

*So Abraham took the wood of the burnt offering and laid it on Isaac his son; and he took the fire in his hand, and a knife, and the two of them went together. But Isaac spoke to Abraham his father and said, "My father!" And he said, "Here I am, my son." Then he said, "Look, the fire and the wood, but where is the lamb for a burnt offering?" **And Abraham said, "My son, God will provide for Himself the lamb for a burnt offering."** (Genesis 22:6–8, emphasis added)*

F.   The perfect Son of God became a perfectly qualified man through the things He endured. It was through suffering that Christ pioneered a path into unbroken communion and access to the fullness of the knowledge of God.

*Jesus said to him, "I am the way, the truth, and the life. **No one comes to the Father except through Me."** (John 14:6, emphasis added)*

. . . And raised us up together, and made us sit together in the heavenly places in Christ Jesus . . . (Ephesians 2:6)

To them God willed to make known what are the riches of the glory of this mystery among the Gentiles: which is Christ in you, the hope of glory. (Colossians 1:27)

G.   The knowledge of God is not something that we automatically receive along with salvation, but rather it is the gift of God dispensed and administrated by the Son of God. We receive the knowledge of God by putting our hearts before the Lord Jesus and asking Him to declare the name of God that we may be filled with the knowledge of His will. Jesus' work on the earth was to glorify the Father. He accomplished this by revealing Him through word and deed.

H.   The Cross of Christ is a stumbling block and foolishness (1 Corinthians 1:23) when we consider the cruelty and ugliness of the cross upon which One as beautiful as Jesus died. Yet, it is the pinnacle of Jesus' glorification—the height of humility, power, wisdom, love, compassion and justice are expressed in it. The Cross is also our invitation and entrance into the heights of the knowledge of this glory (Romans 5:2). It is the only way to experience life. The gateway to the Kingdom of God is living the life of the Cross.

I.   The issue that was on the forefront of Jesus' mind on His way to the cross was the knowledge of God and bringing humanity into that reality. God, in His perfect wisdom, conceived of the idea of the slain Lamb before the foundation of the earth. The very depth of God's creative and manifold wisdom was displayed in dreaming up the plan to converge Heaven and Earth and fill them with His fullness. In this context, He will dwell forever with humanity who, empowered by the Resurrection accomplished after the Cross, would freely choose to love God forever.

J.   In Hebrews 6:19–20, the writer tells us that Christ was the forerunner who went beyond the veil into His Presence. This is in keeping with Christ's request to enter again into the fullness of the glory He possessed with the Father—but now as One who is fully God **and** fully Man. Through the Cross, He went beyond the veil that we might enter in with Him forever.

     And the glory which You gave Me I have given them, that they may be one just as We are one . . . (John 17:22)

     This hope we have as an anchor of the soul, both sure and steadfast, and which **enters the Presence behind the veil, where the forerunner has entered for us, even Jesus**, *having become High Priest forever according to the order of Melchizedek. (Hebrews 6:19–20, emphasis added)*

K. The zeal of Christ that drove Him to the cross was and is the glory of His Father. Jesus fought for the honor of His Father even unto death, that the Father would have His honor in Heaven and on Earth forever.

L. **John 17:5** expresses Christ's desire to be swallowed up in the Godhead again forever. This glorification would involve going to the cross. It was the joy set before Him.

I have manifested Your name to the men whom You have given Me out of the world. They were Yours, You gave them to Me, and they have kept Your word. (John 17:6)

III. THE KNOWLEDGE OF GOD: THE MISSION OF CHRIST JESUS (JOHN 17:6–8)

A. Jesus declares to us in a more specific manner the nature of His mission on the earth. The mandate of Christ is the knowledge of God. The central issue is that Christ came to Earth to make visible and clear the truth concerning His Father. This is still His central mission. The One who was hidden in the bosom of the Father is the One who made the Father manifest. This will happen ultimately when the full reconciliation of Heaven and Earth, made possible through the Cross, is made manifest unto God releasing the fullness of His personality in Heaven and on the earth.

*. . . Having made known to us **the mystery of His will**, according to His good pleasure which He purposed in Himself, that in the dispensation of the fullness of the times **He might gather together in one all things in Christ, both which are in heaven and which are on earth—in Him.** (Ephesians 1:9–10, emphasis added)*

*For it pleased the Father that **in Him all the fullness should dwell**, and by Him to **reconcile** all things to Himself, by Him, whether **things on earth or things in heaven**, having made peace through the blood of His cross. (Colossians 1:19–20, emphasis added)*

B. The Second Person is forever in the embrace of the Father in eternity– God searching God. This wealth of glory is what the seraphim around the Throne call holy or transcendent majesty. God enjoying God, God stunned by the beauty of God, God searching out God, and God desiring that, in the very center of redemption, the Holy Spirit would usher humans into this reality through the Cross of Christ Jesus. This was Christ's mission: to make clear the heart and the truth of God to human hearts.

C.   Paul's prayer for the Ephesians in 1:17 of his letter to them is that they be surrounded by the realm of the knowledge of God while Colossians 1:9 is a prayer to be filled with the knowledge of His will. There is such power in the inner man when Christ Jesus manifests the name of the Father in us by the Third Person of the Trinity. This is what we were created for. In John 17:5, Jesus refers to the glory that He possessed with the Father before the foundations of the earth. It is from that reality that He came to the earth, laid aside the form of God, and took on the form of a man to reveal the knowledge of God. It is so amazing to think that God's purpose for making all things was for divine self-disclosure. What is even more stunning is that the only way it would be valuable to Him is if real choices and real decisions were involved so that humanity's love back to Him would indeed be love—voluntary, not compelled. It is only in the context of real choices that the full extent of God's love can be revealed and love for God can be cultivated.

. . . That the God of our Lord Jesus Christ, the Father of glory, may give to you the spirit of wisdom and revelation in the knowledge of Him . . . (Ephesians 1:17)

*For this reason we also, since the day we heard it, do not cease to pray for you, and to ask that you may be **filled with the knowledge of His will** in all wisdom and spiritual understanding . . . (Colossians 1:9, emphasis added)*

*. . . **The mystery which has been hidden from ages and from generations, but now has been revealed to His saints.** To them God willed to make known what are the riches of **the glory of this mystery** among the Gentiles: which is **Christ in you, the hope of glory.** (Colossians 1:26–27, emphasis added)*

D.   God knew that in giving humanity choices sin would enter. However, even this fits within His perfect plan. His coming to broken, rebellious humanity and revealing the height of His love through the Cross of Christ fully dealt with the problem of sin. Christ came in the fullness of time to bring redemption. This means that He came during the optimum conditions in which the height of God's love could be expressed.

*But when **the fullness of the time had come** (the conditions were optimum from the perspective of the divine counsels), God sent forth His Son, born of a woman, born under the law, to redeem those who were under the law, **that we might receive the adoption as sons*** (God wants sons). *(Galatians 4:4–5, emphasis and parenthetical comments added)*

E.   The highest manifestation of God's name is in the thunder of His passion, which is revealed at the Cross. Christ came to manifest the very nature of God's love in that God is love. When Christ reveals the name of the Father, the reality, the power, and the mystery of true love are revealed to the human heart. This revelation ignites our souls and sets us on fire. In the name of God we see the personality, plans, purposes and depths of God's fiery affections for humans.

F.   Here, Jesus gives us a very powerful vision and reality for true ministry. Jesus' disciples were **given** to Him by the Father. They **belonged** to the Father and were **entrusted** to the Son of God for the **sole** purpose of manifesting the knowledge of God to them. The same is true today. The entrustments (people) that the Lord gives us are for the purpose of pointing us to the knowledge of God. The knowledge of God is more than a subject; it is a reality in the Spirit.

G.   Christ was able to manifest the name of the Father because He dwelt in the glory of God forever in eternity past. The knowledge of God can only be shared in as much as we give ourselves to experiencing the embrace of the Father in the knowledge of Him through long and loving encounters with Him. It is crucial in this hour of history that leaders throw themselves into the depths of the knowledge of God. Leaders must have undistracted focus if they want to go deep into the realm of the knowledge of God in Christ Jesus.

IV.   HOLINESS: THE CONTAINER OF THE KNOWLEDGE OF GOD

A.   Jesus declared that the disciples received and kept the words concerning the Father that He gave to them. As Christ gives us the knowledge of God, we too must give a diligent watch over the Word of God. Christ's mission was not just to impart of the knowledge of God, but also to equip and train His disciples to maintain and grow in that knowledge. Pursuit of the Sermon on the Mount lifestyle allows us to grow in the knowledge of God, and we keep it by a lifestyle that produces encounter. It is not just a matter of study, though study is a vital part of the pursuit of the knowledge of God. The knowledge of God is kept as **we aggressively pursue lives of one hundred percent obedience in the grace of God.** We cannot obtain one hundred percent obedience in this life, but the pursuit of holiness is what counts in God's eyes.

But also for this very reason, giving all diligence, add to your faith virtue, to virtue knowledge, to knowledge self-control, to self-control perseverance, to perseverance godliness, to godliness brotherly kindness, and to brotherly kindness love. For if these things are yours and abound, you will be neither barren nor unfruitful in the knowledge of our Lord Jesus Christ. (2 Peter 1:5–8)

1.   "Add to your faith": Hebrews 11—the gift of God that connects us with eternity.

2.   "To your faith virtue": moral excellence, i.e., eyes and speech.

3.   "To virtue knowledge": the knowledge of God.

4.   "To knowledge self-control": self-government over one's soul and its desires.

5.   "To self-control perseverance": persistence in the context of the oppositions of life.

6.   "To perseverance godliness": living a devout life, the fasted lifestyle and spiritual disciplines.

7.   "To godliness brotherly kindness": the reality of affection and favor fitting for brothers.

8.   "To brotherly kindness love": strong affection with personal ties.

B.   That the disciples kept the word of God means that they were responsive to the knowledge of God in pursuing Jesus toward one hundred percent obedience. The disciples were not by any means perfect, which is a clearly established point throughout the gospels. Rather, they were men who threw themselves fully into the embrace of Christ Jesus. They said "Yes!"

V.   ALL THINGS BELONG TO JESUS

Now they have known that all things which You have given Me are from You. For I have given to them the words which You have given Me; and they have received them, and have known surely that I came forth from You; and they have believed that You sent Me. (John 17:7–8)

A.   All things belong to Jesus. The Man Christ Jesus is the One the Father appointed to be heir of all things (Hebrews 1:2). It is crucial to understand and embrace this divine appointment. Understanding the Father's delegation of authority and leadership to Jesus enables us to understand with whom we are dealing and who is calling us to rule and reign with Him in love. Jesus is the Christ. He is God's Anointed. He is God's King who is to rule and administrate the affairs of God's divine empire.

B.   The knowledge of God drives us into receiving and understanding the revelation of Christ. When we run into the heart of the Father, we see Christ; in the heart of Christ, we see the glory of the Father: the Spirit of God escorting us into the depth of the Divine, contemplating the Divine.

C.   **John 17:7** starts out with "Now," which shows us the process of Christ manifesting the name of the Father (knowledge of God), causing the disciples to understand Christ. All authority in Heaven and on Earth has been given to this Man. This reality should cause us to tremble before Him in humble surrender and loving adoration.

D.   In **John 17:8,** we see that Jesus was given the decrees of the Father, and He gave them to His disciples. The words of the Father resulted in the revelation of Jesus. This is similar in some ways to Revelation chapter 1 where the Father grants Jesus permission to give the Revelation of Christ to the Church. Oh, that the words we speak would usher others into the realm of the knowledge of God and the Lordship of Christ Jesus.

*Then I looked, and I heard the voice of many angels around the throne, the living creatures, and the elders; and the number of them was ten thousand times ten thousand, and thousands of thousands, saying with a loud voice: "**Worthy** is the Lamb who was slain **to receive** power and riches and wisdom, and strength and honor and glory and blessing!" (Revelation 5:11–12, emphasis added)*

Session Five: The Existence of God and the Sin of Humanity

I.   THE ORIGIN OF GOD

    A.   God is uncreated, and He stands alone. He has no origin, in that He exists on His own and is sustained by Himself. God has no source but God, and He has no medium whatsoever to provide sustenance for Him but Himself.

    B.   Nothing or no one caused God to come forth. There was not a time when God began. He has always been and will always be. This is a very difficult concept for us to grasp because everything finite has a beginning.

    C.   *Whatever exists must have had a cause that antedates it and was at least equal to it, since the lesser cannot produce the greater. Any person or thing may be at once both caused and the cause of someone or something else; and so, back to the One who is the cause of all but is Himself caused by none.*[1]

         *. . . Having made known to us the mystery of His will, according to His good pleasure which **He purposed in Himself** . . . (Ephesians 1:9, emphasis added)*

    D.   God is the ultimate original and unique One, finding inspiration within Himself for forming and executing His eternal purposes, whereas humans find inspiration outside themselves. God has need of nothing and nobody—He is self-existing and self-sufficient.

    E.   God is original and is His own origin. He needs nothing to exist or be sustained.

         *"I am **the Alpha and the Omega, the Beginning and the End**," says the Lord, "who is and who was and who is to come, the Almighty." (Revelation 1:8, emphasis added)*

         *Who has performed and done it, calling the generations from the beginning? "I, the L*ord*, am **the first; and with the last I am He.**" (Isaiah 41:4, emphasis added)*

---

1   Tozer, A.W. *The Knowledge of the Holy* (San Francisco: HarperSanFrancisco, 1961), p. 25.

II. **DENYING THE EXISTENCE OF GOD**

A. Denying the existence of God is done by embracing an atheistic philosophy or by the practice of atheism.

B. The ultimate issue of sin is denial of God's existence. This is the root out of which all evil grows. Another word for sin could be pride. All evil flows out of pride, which is the exaltation of self above everything that is called God.

Let no one deceive you by any means; for that Day will not come unless the falling away comes first, and the man of sin is revealed, **the son of perdition, who opposes and exalts himself above all that is called God** *or that is worshiped, so that he sits as God in the temple of God,* **showing himself that he is God.** *(2 Thessalonians 2:3–4, emphasis added)*

C. The nature of sin is the denial of God and choosing anything other than God. Sin came into being when Satan chose himself as supreme. Sin entered into creation when Adam and Eve responded to Satan's temptation and they chose themselves above God. The problem with sin is self. Therefore, Jesus declares fierce war on our egotism.

When He had called the people to Himself, with His disciples also, He said to them, "Whoever desires to come after Me, **let him deny himself, and take up his cross, and follow Me. For whoever desires to save his life will lose it, but whoever loses his life for My sake and the gospel's will save it.** *For what will it profit a man if he gains the whole world, and loses his own soul?* **Or what will a man give in exchange for his soul?"** *(Mark 8:34–37, emphasis added)*

D. *I believe that sin is rooted in selfishness even when it does not result in personal benefit. Since our sinful actions do not carbon copy God's agenda for us, then any action or attitude that contradicts the character of God is a selfish attempt to take control of life.*[2]

E. Question: If God has always been and if God always existed, where did sin come from? If God made everything, did He create sin?

F. God did not create sin, but He gives His creation choice. This is because He wants the rule of His kingdom to be love, and love cannot exist without the glorious operation of choice. God gives us the choice to either follow Him in love or choose ourselves above Him. The choosing of self above God is what gives birth to sin.

---

2   Gamez, Cesar. http://www.cesargamez.com.

G.   *Sin had its origin in a principle of negation, which means that it is not the result of any positive force. Moral beings were created good, but not immutably and independently good. This would have made them equal with God; it would have involved the absurdity of God creating another God. God alone is immutable and independent. There cannot be more than one God, self-existent and self-sufficient, sovereign and supreme.*[3]

H.   *Moral beings, angels and man, were dependent upon God in remaining good. A sustaining power must continually go out from God if moral creatures continue as created. "Which holdeth our soul in life, and suffereth not our feet to be moved" (#Ps 66:9); "For in him we live, and move, and have our being; as certain also of your own poets have said, For we are also his offspring" (#Ac 17:28); "For by him were all things created, that are in heaven, and that are in earth, visible and invisible, whether they be thrones, or dominions, or principalities, or powers: all things were created by him, and for him: And he is before all things, and by him all things consist" (#Col 1:16,17); "Who being the brightness of his glory, and the express image of his person, and upholding all things by the word of his power, when he had by himself purged our sins, sat down on the right hand of the Majesty on high:" (Heb 1:3).*[4]

I.   *The definition of sin is fallen selfhood. God made us to be like planets—around and around they go, held by the magnetic attraction of the sun... Then one day the little planet said, "I'll be my own sun. Away with this God." And man fell. That's what we call the fall of man. That's where sin came in—sin reached up and took God's self and said, I'll be self myself. And God was ruled out.*[5]

J.   Sin was not created, but rather entered into creation when we denied God and lifted up self as God. The evil in the world today is but the manifestation of sin. Lust, greed, envy, etc. are all manifestations of the atheism of our heart. A heart that dethrones God and exalts self is a heart prone to all manner of iniquity. Atheism is more a matter of the heart than a matter of the mind. **"Men may have atheistical hearts without atheistical heads. Their reasons may defend the notion of a Deity, while their hearts are empty of affection to the Deity."**[6]

3   Cole, C.D. "The Origin of Sin." Agape Chapel Ministries, http://sounddoctrine.net/LIBRARY/Modern_Day_Reform_Teaching/C.D.%20Cole/origin_sin.htm.
4   Ibid.
5   Tozer, A.W. *The Attributes of God, Volume Two* (Camp Hill: Wing Spread, 2007), p. 27.
6   Charnock, Stephen. *The Existence and Attributes of God, Volume One* (Grand Rapids: Baker Books, 2005), p. 89. Emphasis added.

K.   *Sin has symptoms and manifestations, just as cancer has certain manifestations . . . Sin also has manifestations–many manifestations. Paul gives a list of them in Galatians 5:19-21: "Now the works of the flesh are manifest, which are these; Adultery, fornication, uncleanness, lasciviousness, idolatry, witchcraft, hatred, variance, emulations, wrath, strife, seditions, heresies, envyings, murders, drunkenness, revellings, and such like."*[7]

III.   THE KNOWLEDGE OF GOD: THE DIVINE PRESENCE THAT COMBATS SIN IN THE HUMAN HEART

And this is eternal life, that they may know You, the only true God, and Jesus Christ whom You have sent. (John 17:3)

A.   Growing in the knowledge of God is the root source of power over sin in our lives because sin is related to the absence of the knowledge of God or the presence of atheism in the human heart.

B.   The divine presence is that which combats sin in the human heart. The way that the heart is liberated from sin is by exposing our hearts to the subject of the knowledge of God.

*The fool has **said in his heart, "There is no God." They are corrupt, and have done abominable iniquity;** there is none who does good. (Psalm 53:1, emphasis added)*

C.   The knowledge of God—the presence and the existence of God manifested in the human soul—releases His grace and power for life and godliness.

*To them **God willed to make known** what are the riches of the glory of this mystery among the Gentiles: which is Christ **in you**, the hope of glory. (Colossians 1:27, emphasis added)*

*But he who is joined to the Lord is **one spirit with Him.** (1 Corinthians 6:17, emphasis added)*

---

7   Ibid., p. 28.

> *Grace and peace be multiplied to you in the knowledge of God and of Jesus our Lord, as **His divine power has given to us all things that pertain to life and godliness, through the knowledge of Him** who called us by glory and virtue, by which have been given to us exceedingly great and precious promises, that through these **you may be partakers of the divine nature**, having escaped the corruption that is in the world through lust. (2 Peter 1:2–4, emphasis added)*

D. The knowledge of God is Jesus' strategy to awaken fiery affection in the heart of the Bride of Christ for Himself.

> ***And I have declared to them Your name, and will declare it***, *that the love with which You loved Me may be in them, and I in them. (John 17:26, emphasis added)*

> *In that day the Branch of the LORD shall be beautiful and glorious . . . (Isaiah 4:2)*

Session Six: God Incomprehensible—The Width, the Length, the Depth, the Height

I.   **GOD IS BEYOND OUR ABILITY TO UNDERSTAND**

> *To me, who am less than the least of all the saints, this grace was given, that I should preach among the Gentiles **the unsearchable riches of Christ**... (Ephesians 3:8, emphasis added)*

> ***Oh, the depth of the riches** both of the wisdom and knowledge of God! **How unsearchable** are His judgments and **His ways past finding out!** "For who has known the mind of the LORD? Or who has become His counselor? Or who has first given to Him and it shall be repaid to him?" **For of Him and through Him and to Him are all things, to whom be glory forever. Amen.** (Romans 11:33–36, emphasis added)*

A.   The uncreated God is filled with mystery, and the day that the mystery leaves Him is the day He ceases to be God. In his first letter to the Corinthians, the Apostle Paul tells us that in eternity God will still be searching God.

B.   God is incomprehensible in that He cannot be comprehended by the natural mind. Hence, we need the aiding of the spirit of revelation to comprehend Him.

> *But God has revealed them to us through His Spirit. For the Spirit **searches** (present tense) all things, yes, the deep things of God. (1 Corinthians 2:10, emphasis and parenthetical comment added)*

C.   God is not exactly like anything or anybody. He is not a concept, but a real being and person. God cannot be conceptualized, in that even the loftiest thought that we can have of him falls infinitely short of describing who He is and what He is truly like.

D.   *We learn by using what we already know as a bridge over which we pass to the unknown. It is not possible for the mind to crash suddenly past the familiar into the totally unfamiliar. Even the most vigorous and daring mind is unable to create something out of nothing by a spontaneous act of the imagination.[1]*

---

1   Tozer, A.W. *The Knowledge of the Holy* (San Francisco: HarperSanFrancisco, 1961), p. 6.

II.   GOD IS INDESCRIBABLE

A.   When speaking of God incomprehensible, we are speaking of the glory of God's being as He is shrouded in mystery. The uncreated God is filled with mystery and the day the mystery leaves Him is the day he ceases to be God.

B.   *The divine radiance and loveliness are so endlessly beyond anything we can imagine or experience that revelation chooses a special term to speak of it. That term is* glory, *a word that occurs repeatedly in Scripture.*[2]

Thanks be to God for His indescribable gift! (2 Corinthians 9:15)

C.   Many times throughout the Word, God's messengers have had to lean on simile in order to describe Him. A simile is a figure of speech used to draw a comparison between two things that are unlike each other. Such descriptions are often introduced by the word "like."

*And He who sat there was **like** a jasper and a sardius stone in appearance; and there was a rainbow around the throne, in appearance **like** an emerald. (Revelation 4:3, emphasis added)*

D.   *So, in order to convey an idea of what he sees, the prophet must employ such words as 'likeness,' 'appearance,' 'as it were,' and 'the likeness of the appearance.' Even the throne becomes 'the appearance of a throne' and He that sits upon it, though like a man, is so* unlike *one that He can be described only as 'the likeness of the appearance of a man.'*[3]

E.   To say that God is indescribable means that we cannot imagine or fathom His being or what He is like. He cannot be contained in the finitude of our minds. He cannot be conceptualized in that even the loftiest thought that we can have of Him falls infinitely short of describing who He is and what He is truly like. God is infinitely beyond anything that we can imagine.

F.   Thomas Dubay says, "We can authentically know him but must always understand that he is infinitely more than even our accurate and best ideas can express."[4] God can only be understood in as much as God reveals God to the human heart.

---

2   Dubay, Thomas. *The Evidential Power of Beauty* (San Francisco: Ignatius, 1999), p. 296.
3   Tozer, A.W. *The Knowledge of the Holy* (San Francisco: HarperSanFrancisco, 1961), p. 7.
4   Dubay, Thomas. *The Evidential Power of Beauty* (San Francisco: Ignatius, 1999), p. 295.

*Who does great things, and **unsearchable**, marvelous things without number. (Job 5:9, emphasis added)*

***Can you search out the deep things of God? Can you find out the limits of the Almighty?** They are higher than heaven— what can you do? Deeper than Sheol— what can you know? Their measure is longer than the earth and broader than the sea. (Job 11:7–8, emphasis added)*

*God thunders marvelously with His voice; He does great things which **we cannot comprehend.** (Job 37:5, emphasis added)*

Great is the LORD, and greatly to be praised; and His greatness is unsearchable. (Psalm 145:3)

*And the light shines in the darkness, and **the darkness did not comprehend it.** (John 1:5, emphasis added)*

*. . . To know **the love of Christ which passes knowledge**; that you may be filled with all the fullness of God. Now to Him who is able to do **exceedingly abundantly above all that we ask or think**, according to the power that works in us . . . (Ephesians 3:19–20, emphasis added)*

*Be anxious for nothing, but in everything by prayer and supplication, with thanksgiving, let your requests be made known to God; and **the peace of God, which surpasses all understanding**, will guard your hearts and minds through Christ Jesus. (Philippians 4:6–7, emphasis added)*

G.   *For centuries philosophers and theologians have discussed and analyzed this problem: correctly speaking about what really cannot be spoken, intelligently discussing that which is far beyond any human image, idea, or words. Their solution is called analogy, and it tells us how we, created, finite, limited beings, bridge the infinite gap between us and our unlimited Creator and somehow grasp him who is endlessly beyond our best concepts. On the one hand we must have some link with him, given that he brought us into being. We must be somehow like to him, somehow similar.[5]*

H.   We can only understand God in as much as He reveals Himself through the Holy Spirit. God in all of His vastness cannot be grasped or understood by the natural mind. The knowledge of God is not a given; rather, it is a gift.

---

5   Dubay, Thomas. *The Evidential Power of Beauty* (San Francisco: Ignatius, 1999), p. 294–295.

*These things we also speak, not in words which man's wisdom teaches but which the Holy Spirit teaches, comparing spiritual things with spiritual. **But the natural man does not receive the things of the Spirit of God, for they are foolishness to him;** nor can he know them, because **they are spiritually discerned.** But he who is spiritual judges all things, yet he himself is rightly judged by no one. For "who has known the mind of the LORD that he may instruct Him?" **But we** (corporate dynamic) **have the mind of Christ.** (1 Corinthians 2:13–16, emphasis and parenthetical comment added)*

*Jesus answered and said to him, "Blessed are you, Simon Bar-Jonah, **for flesh and blood has not revealed** this to you, but My Father who is in heaven. (Matthew 16:17, emphasis added)*

I.   Only the Holy Spirit can give us the ability to comprehend the incomprehensible. Embracing the reality of the incomprehensible love and beauty of God has a corporate dynamic.

III.   GLORY SUPREME: HE WHO HAS SEEN THE SON HAS SEEN THE FATHER

A.   The revelation of God through the prophets was fragmented and partial. They were whispers compared to the thunder of revelation that came through the Son of God. Christ is the only One who could make God known in full. Christ came to make in the incomprehensible known.

B.   God spoke His final and decisive decree through Christ. All that God has to say about Himself is proclaimed in and through the Person of Christ.

*God, who at various times and in various ways spoke in time past to the fathers by the prophets, has **in these last days spoken to us by His Son,** whom He has appointed heir of all things, through whom also He made the worlds; **who being the brightness of His glory and the express image of His person,** and upholding all things by the word of His power, when He had by Himself purged our sins, sat down at the right hand of the Majesty on high . . . (Hebrews 1:1–3, emphasis added)*

C.   **Christ is the effulgence or the radiance of God's glory.** He is the glory of God, expressing the very character and nature of God's personality.

D.   Revelation of God is displayed in the face of Christ. Jesus is God revealing God to humanity. His radiance is the revelation of God (2 Corinthians 4:6). Jesus is the Light of the world (John 8:12), and He is also the source of revelation inside of us (Colossians 1:27).

E.   *He is the very image and the essence of God. "Jesus is the shining of God's glory amonmen. He says that he was the charactēr of God's very essence. In Greek charactēr means two things, first, a seal, and, second, the impression that the seal leaves on the wax. The impression has the exact form of the seal. So, when the writer to the Hebrews said that Jesus was the charactēr of the being of God, He meant that he was the exact image of God. Just as when you look at the impression, you see exactly what the seal which made it is like, so when you look at Jesus you see exactly what God is like."[6]*

F.   The very nature of the character of God is stamped upon the nature and essence of Christ. Just as the glory of God is reflected in Christ, so the being of God is truly in Him as well. It pleased the Father that the fullness should dwell in Him (Colossians 1:19; 2:9).

IV.   MYSTERY: CHRIST IN YOU THE HOPE OF GLORY

A.   The reality of the mystery of the Gospel is that it is hidden in the heart of God in Christ. Christ reveals the incomprehensible to us by the Spirit of God dwelling inside the spirit of the redeemed. Information concerning the mystery is found all throughout the Word of God and must be sought after like one searching for a pearl of great price.

It is the glory of God to conceal a matter, but the glory of kings is to search out a matter. (Proverbs 25:2)

B.   A principle of the kingdom is that God gives more to the **hungry.** We are to pursue the revelation of the knowledge of God with all our heart, mind, soul and strength. The glory, the wisdom and the beauty of the mystery of God are hidden, but they are progressively made plain to the hungry.

---

6   Barclay, William. *The Letter to the Hebrews.* The Daily Study Bible series, rev. ed. (The Westminster Press: Philadelphia, 2000, c. 1975), as quoted in *Scholar's Library: Silver* (Logos Bible Software: 2004). Emphasis added.

*For I want you to know what a great conflict I have for you and those in Laodicea, and for as many as have not seen my face in the flesh, that their hearts may be **encouraged**, being **knit together in love**, and **attaining to all riches of the full assurance** of understanding, **to the knowledge of the mystery of God**, both of the Father and of Christ, **in whom are hidden all the treasures of wisdom and knowledge**. (Colossians 2:1–3, emphasis added)*

C.   Christ dwelling in us by the Holy Spirit is also a promissory note of the fullness of the knowledge of God (Colossians 1:20; Ephesians 1:13).

*To them God has chosen to make known among the Gentiles the glorious riches of this mystery, which is **Christ in you, the hope of glory.** (Colossians 1:27, NIV, emphasis added)*

D.   This reality of the indwelling Spirit is one of the great mysteries of the **new thing** that God spoke of in the Old Testament.

*Behold, the former things have come to pass, **and new things I declare;** before they spring forth I tell you of them. (Isaiah 42:9, emphasis added)*

*Do not remember the former things, nor consider the things of old. **Behold, I will do a new thing**, now it shall spring forth; **shall you not know it?** (Isaiah 43:18–19, emphasis added)*

E.   The **indwelling** of God is one of the foundational realities of the New Covenant.

*Then I will give them one heart, and **I will put a new spirit within them**, and take the stony heart out of their flesh, and give them a heart of flesh, that they may walk in My statutes and keep My judgments and do them; and **they shall be My people, and I will be their God.** (Ezekiel 11:19–20, emphasis added)*

*"Behold, the days are coming," says the LORD, "when **I will make a new covenant** with the house of Israel and with the house of Judah—**not according to the covenant that I made with their fathers** in the day that I took them by the hand to lead them out of the land of Egypt, **My covenant which they broke, though I was a husband to them**," says the LORD. "But this is the covenant that I will make with the house of Israel after those days," says the LORD: "**I will put My law in their minds, and write it on their hearts; and I will be their God, and they shall be My people** (the covenant formula of Revelation 21:3). No more shall every man teach his neighbor, and every man his brother, saying, 'Know the LORD,' for **they all shall know Me, from the least of them to the greatest of them**," says the LORD. "For I will forgive their iniquity, and their sin I will remember no more." (Jeremiah 31:31–34, emphasis and parenthetical comment added)*

Cast away *from you all the transgressions which you have committed, and **get yourselves a new heart and a new spirit.** For why should you die, O house of Israel? (Ezekiel 18:31, emphasis added)*

F. Our being is indwelled by God; therefore, our mind and emotions are illumined, enlarged and empowered by the Spirit. The Holy Spirit gives us new **capacities** for love and righteousness—the fullness of God. The mystery is that we get the capacity to contain God but we **never** become God. We will always be redeemed humanity, but God so fills us with Himself that our thinking and our emotions will be **energized** by the fullness of the Spirit.

G. We will have the mind of Christ, being able to think His thoughts without becoming omniscient. Omniscience is an attribute that only belongs to the Godhead, but we will have portions imparted to us. We will be able to experience the love the Father has for His Son. **In eternity, we will walk around with our humanity glorified by the indwelling God resident within us.**

H. We who once were dirty creatures who rebelled against God, who lived in perversion, who were filled with demons, are now able to walk and move with the living God who is living and moving and having **expression** in our humanity. 2 Peter 1:4 calls it "the Divine nature." **In eternity, will be able to think and feel like God.**

*Whoever has been born of God does not sin, **for His seed** (sperma) **remains in him**; and he cannot sin, because he has been born of God. (1 John 3:9, emphasis and parenthetical comment added)*

For "who has known the mind of the LORD that he may instruct Him?" **But we have the mind of Christ.** *(1 Corinthians 2:16, emphasis added)*

I.   The eternal plan of the Father is to have an eternal **partner** for His Son who will understand Him and speak in a way that even satisfies His heart beyond anything we can imagine.

Thus says the LORD: "Let not the wise man glory in his wisdom, let not the mighty man glory in his might, nor let the rich man glory in his riches; But let him who glories glory in this, **that he understands and knows Me**, *that I am the LORD, exercising lovingkindness, judgment, and righteousness in the earth.* **For in these I delight**," *says the LORD. (Jeremiah 9:23–24, emphasis added)*

J.   The indwelling Spirit means that we will **rule** as He rules. We will speak and things will come into order under His leadership. Our words have **creative** power, the full capacity for revelation and the capacity for holy emotions (love). Everything we do will be from the motivation of this unending love. We are so motivated as God is because He dwells in us in fullness.

To this end I also labor, striving according to His working which works in me mightily. (Colossians 1:29)

If you **abide in Me, and My words abide in you, you will ask what you desire**, *and it shall be done for you. (John 15:7, emphasis added)*

You will make your prayer to Him, He will hear you, and you will pay your vows. **You will also declare a thing, and it will be established for you**; *So light will shine on your ways. (Job 22:27–28, emphasis added)*

K.   Our spirit will be impacted with the fullness of the nine fruits of the Spirit in our thinking and our emotions.

Session Seven: The Emotions of God

I. **THE EMOTIONS OF GOD: TRANSCENDENT AND DIVINE**

   A. The doctrine of the emotions of God is not a system of anthropomorphic language, as though God has human emotions. The emotions of God are divine and transcendent in nature. They are spiritual.

   B. All of God's emotions are deep and matchless expressions of His divine being and essence; for example, love, wrath, jealousy, joy, and grief. God's emotions are not soulish but spiritual, and they can be powerfully experienced in the heart of the born again believer.

   "For My thoughts are not your thoughts, nor are your ways My ways," says the LORD. "For as the heavens are higher than the earth, so are My ways higher than your ways, and My thoughts than your thoughts." (Isaiah 55:8–9, emphasis added)

II. **THE CROSS: THE BEGINNING OF THE EMOTIONS OF GOD**

   A. The revelation of true love and affection is revealed in the realm of the Cross. This is the beginning point for pursuing understanding of the emotions of God.

   B. Without the revelation of the Cross, we will approach this doctrine of the pathos, or the divine emotions, of God from our own sensuality, thus making the Bridal Paradigm sensual.

   *Who is wise and understanding among you? Let him show by good conduct that his works are done in the meekness of wisdom. But if you have **bitter envy and self-seeking** in your hearts, do not boast and lie against the truth. **This wisdom** does not descend from above, but **is earthly, sensual, demonic.** For where envy and self-seeking exist, confusion and every evil thing are there. (James 3:13–16, emphasis added)*

   C. Today, most of our experience in the realm of the soul is self-seeking surges that look to be satisfied in the lifting of our souls to another, the worship of a God created in our own image. As a result, we are tempted to relate to God on the same basis, as though His emotions are like ours.

D.   Being sensual refers to our preoccupation with secondary, earthly pleasures (both legitimate and illegitimate) to satisfy our appetites.

E.   Studying the Cross focuses us on eternal things instead of lesser, temporal things. The Cross of Christ gives us profound insight into the deep things of God because the Cross is the very center of who He is.

III.   GOD IS CAPABLE OF EMOTION

A.   One of the most powerful realities in Christianity is that we do not have an apathetic God. We serve a God who we not only experience, but who also experiences us.

*You have **ravished** My heart, My sister, My spouse; you have **ravished** My heart with **one look of your eyes**, with one link of your necklace. (Song of Solomon 4:9, emphasis added)*

*For as a young man marries a virgin, so shall your sons marry you; and **as the bridegroom rejoices over the bride, so shall your God rejoice over you**. (Isaiah 62:5, emphasis added)*

*The Lord your God in your midst, the Mighty One, will save; He will rejoice over you with gladness, He will quiet you with His love, **He will rejoice over you with singing**. (Zephaniah 3:17, emphasis added)*

B.   The word "ravish" means to seize and **take away by violence**; to overcome with emotion (as joy or delight).[1]

*And from the days of John the Baptist until now **the kingdom of heaven suffers violence**, and the violent take it by force. (Matthew 11:12, emphasis added)*

*Turn **your eyes** away from me, for **they have overcome me** . . . (Song of Solomon 6:5, emphasis added)*

C.   We do not just experience God. God experiences us. The weak yet deepest reaches of our heart toward Christ Jesus affect the heart of God, and He moves toward us accordingly.

Draw near to God and He will draw near to you. (James 4:8)

*Come, and **let us return to the Lord**; for He has torn, but **He will** heal us; He has stricken, but **He will** bind us up. (Hosea 6:1, emphasis added)*

---

1   "Ravish." Dictionary.com. *Dictionary.com Unabridged (v 1.1)*. Random House, Inc., http://. dictionary.reference.com.

D.   Edmond La B. Cherbonnier quotes Abraham Herschel's *The Prophets, Volume Two*, which states: "[God] is moved and affected by what happens in the world, and reacts accordingly."[2]

E.   Many people throughout history have viewed God as stoic. A stoic is somehow indifferent to the experience of emotions, especially emotions associated with pain.

F.   *In most philosophies, the conception of God serves as the model toward which human beings should aspire.* **Since the God of the philosophers is emotionally neutral, it is not surprising that the ideal human being is also conceived in the same way.** *For the Stoics, the ideal was not pathos but its opposite, apathy;* **for Spinoza, human emotions represented a kind of bondage** *from which philosophy could liberate the intelligent few;* **for Immanuel Kant, "the wise man must never succumb to emotions, even to that of sympathy for the evils which befall his best friend."** *For most philosophers, therefore, prophetic sympathy, like divine pathos, is irrational.*[3]

G.   The Westminster Confession states:

       1.   *There is but one only living and true God, who is infinite in being and perfection, a most pure spirit, invisible,* ***without body, parts, or passions;*** *immutable, immense, eternal, incomprehensible, almighty, most wise, most holy, most free, most absolute; working all things according to the counsel of his own immutable and most righteous will, for his own glory; most loving, gracious, merciful, long-suffering, abundant in goodness and truth, forgiving iniquity, transgression and sin; the rewarder of them that diligently seek Him; and withal, most just, and terrible in His judgements, hating all sin, and who will by no means clear the guilty.*[4]

H.   The Confession affirms that God is "without body, parts or passions…"[5]

---

2   Cherbonnier, Edmond La B. "Divine Pathos and Prophetic Sympathy." Philosophy and Religion, http://www.philosophy-religion.org/cherbonnier/divine.htm.

3   Ibid. Emphasis added.

4   The Westminster Confession. The Reformed Churches of New Zealand, http://www.rcnz.org.nz/about/westminster.pdf.

5   Cherbonnier, Edmond La B. "Divine Pathos and Prophetic Sympathy." Philosophy and Religion, http://www.philosophy-religion.org/cherbonnier/divine.htm. Emphasis added.

I.   *It was His essential incapacity for suffering that distinguished God from man and other non-divine beings, all of whom are alike subjected to suffering, as well as to transience and death… But there is third form of suffering: active suffering—the voluntary laying oneself open to another and allowing oneself to be intimately affect by him; that is to say, the suffering of passionate love.*[6]

IV.   THE CHRISTIAN PARADIGM OF GOD[7]

A.   The Christian paradigm of God is founded on the revelation of God's deep emotions of love. The revelation of God as a tender Father and a passionate Bridegroom was a new idea in religious history (see William Barclay's commentary on Hebrews 4).

B.   In Jewish tradition, what was most emphasized about God was that He is holy in the sense of being **totally separate from sin**. They did not think of a holy God as sharing human experience. They thought of God as incapable of sharing it simply because He is God. In other words, they saw God as being above sharing the human dilemma by the very definition of being God.

C.   The Greek philosophers saw God as **emotionally distant** from humans. The most prominent Greek thinkers were the Stoics. They saw the main attribute of God as being *apatheia*, by which they meant God's **inability to feel anything.** They reasoned that if God felt something, then He might be influenced or even controlled by what He felt. They argued that those who felt sorrow or joy were vulnerable to being hurt and thus controlled by those they had feelings for. They believed that anyone who affected God's emotions would be greater than God for that moment. The Epicureans (a school of Greek philosophy) believed that the gods **lived detached** in eternal bliss. They lived in the intermediate world and thus were not aware of events occurring on earth. They were, therefore, totally detached from human affairs as they lived in great happiness.

D.   The Jews understood God as a **holy God** separated from humans; the Stoics a **feeling-less god**; the Epicureans a **detached god**. Into this context of religious thought came the totally new idea of the Christian God who deliberately subjected Himself to human emotion, pain and weakness.

---

6   Moltmann, Jurgen. *The Trinity and the Kingdom*, (Minneapolis: First Fortress Press, 1993), p. 23.

7   Points A–E are taken from one source: Bickle, Mike. 2007. "Song of Solomon: The Ravished Heart of God." The International House of Prayer, http://www.IHOP.org.

E.   It was inconceivable to the religious mindset of the first century that a holy God would have capacity for tenderness, sympathy and affection, who even wrapped Himself in the garments of humanity and then experienced God's wrath on a cross. It is difficult to realize how dramatic this Christian paradigm of God was at that time.

V.   THE DEEP THINGS OF GOD

A.   The uncreated, transcendent God is not apathetic. Rather, He has an infinite capacity to feel deeply, to experience His creation, and to be affected by His creation even to point of suffering grief at the actions of humanity.

B.   *The basic meaning of* πσχη *is "to experience something that comes from outside." At first the "something" is usually bad, and* **while a neutral use develops, the idea of suffering evil remains so strong that an addition is needed to show that good is meant unless the context is very plain.**[8]

C.   *The implication of the above statement is the fact that God can and allows Him to be affected by* **something** *outside Himself. This was contrary to the beliefs of the Stoics who believed that a God who has an ability to be affected emotionally was weak thus saying "The divine substance is incapable of suffering (i.e. feeling grief) otherwise it would not be divine.*[9]

You have ravished My heart, *My sister, My spouse; you have ravished My heart* **with one look of your eyes**, *with one link of your necklace. (Song of Solomon 4:9, emphasis added)*

VI.   AFTER GOD'S OWN HEART

A.   David was a man after God's own heart. This set him apart from all other men and women in the Word of God. There were others who lived extraordinary lives before God in obedience, but David is uniquely recognized throughout the corridors of history because he was a man after God's own heart; David was a student of the emotions of God.

---

8   Kittel, G., Friedrich, G., & Bromiley, G. W. *Theological Dictionary of the New Testament*, translation of: Theologisches Worterbuch zum Neuen Testament (W.B. Eerdmans: Grand Rapids, Mich., 1995, c. 1985), quoted in *Scholar's Library: Silver* (Logos Bible Software: 2004). Emphasis added.

9   Moltmann, Jurgen. *The Trinity and the Kingdom,* (Minneapolis: First Fortress Press, 1993), p. 21. Emphasis added.

B.   Being a man or woman after God's heart refers to a person whose single focus, passion and vision is to pursue and understand the emotions of God. God is not a stale stoic. He is the author of the realm of emotions because He possesses powerful, transcendent emotions within Himself.

C.   A people after God's own heart are those who pursue and encounter the emotions of God that fuel abandonment in their spirits and souls to love Him.

> *Then he said to them, "Go your way, eat the fat, drink the sweet, and send portions to those for whom nothing is prepared; for this day is holy to our LORD. Do not sorrow, for **the joy of the LORD is your strength.***" *(Nehemiah 8:10, emphasis added)*

> *. . . That He would grant you, according to the riches of His glory, **to be strengthened with might through His Spirit in the inner man**, that **Christ may dwell in your hearts** through faith; that you, being **rooted and grounded in love**, may be able to comprehend with all the saints what is the width and length and depth and height— **to know the love of Christ which passes knowledge**; that you may be filled with all the fullness of God. (Ephesians 3:16–19, emphasis added)*

D.   It is vital that we become **students of the emotions of God.** The revelation of God's heart will equip us to become lovesick worshipers. The longer we sit before the fire of God's emotions to encounter and gaze upon them, the more our hearts will be equipped in love, righteousness and holiness.

E.   David was a man who encountered the power of God's emotional makeup. The Psalms are filled with insight into David's spiritual journey after the Lord's heart.

F.   In Psalm 36:8, David describes the heart of God as a rushing river of pleasure and delight, by which we can be abundantly satisfied.

> *You will show me the path of life; in Your presence is fullness of joy; at Your right hand are pleasures forevermore. (Psalm 16:11)*

> *They are **abundantly satisfied** with the fullness of Your house, and **You give them drink from the river of Your pleasures.** (Psalm 36:8, emphasis added)*

G.   Psalm 42:7 describes the heart of God as a mighty waterfall that flows from the very depths of His being.

   Deep calls unto deep *at the noise of Your waterfalls; all Your waves and billows have gone over me. (Psalm 42:7, emphasis added)*

   But God has revealed them to us through His Spirit. For the Spirit searches all things, yes, ***the deep things of God.*** *(Corinthians 2:10, emphasis added)*

VII.   THE PATHOS OF GOD

A.   The pathos of God refers to His ability to express emotions, to feel, and especially His ability to suffer grief.

B.   The doctrine of divine pathos does not speak of a divine attribute, but rather of divine capacity. God is not emotion.

C.   The Jewish theologian, Abraham Heschel, was one of the main advocating voices for the subject of God's emotions, contending against the idea of the apathy of God. He developed the theology of the divine pathos. Jurgen Moltmann points out, "For a long time the divine apathy was a fundamental principle for Jewish theologians too. It was Abraham Heschel who perceived for the first time that the divine pathos is the appropriate hermeneutical point of reference for the anthropomorphic utterance of God in the Old Testament. If we start from the pathos of God, then we do not consider God in His absolute nature, but understand Him in His passion and in His interest in history."[10]

D.   *In his pathos the Almighty goes out of Himself, entering into the people whom He has chosen. He makes Himself a partner in a covenant with His people. In this pathos, this feeling for the people which bears His name and upholds His honor in the world, the Almighty is Himself ultimately affected by Israel's experience, its acts, its sins and its sufferings.* [11]

---

10   Moltmann, Jurgen. *The Trinity and the Kingdom,* (Minneapolis: First Fortress Press, 1993), p. 26.
11   Ibid., p. 25.

Session Eight: The Mystery of the Trinity

I. **THE ATHENASIAN CREED**

A. The Athenasian Creed, so named because it was originally attributed to St. Athanasius, was written to defend the Trinitarian nature of God and the Incarnation of Jesus Christ against Arianism, a heresy that denied the deity of Christ. Arius argued that Christ was not fully divine, was not eternal, and was not begotten of (and thus equal to) the Father. I have divided the creed into several main points:

B. *Whosoever will be saved, before all things it is necessary that he hold the catholic [i.e., universal, Christian] faith. Which faith except everyone does keep whole and undefiled, without doubt he shall perish everlastingly. And the catholic faith is this, that we worship one God in Trinity, and Trinity in Unity; Neither confounding the Persons, nor dividing the Substance. For there is one Person of the Father, another of the Son, and another of the Holy Ghost. But the Godhead of the Father, of the Son, and of the Holy Ghost is all one: the glory equal, the majesty coeternal.*

C. *Such as the Father is, such is the Son, and such is the Holy Ghost. The Father uncreate, the Son uncreate, and the Holy Ghost uncreate. The Father incomprehensible, the Son incomprehensible, and the Holy Ghost incomprehensible. The Father eternal, the Son eternal, and the Holy Ghost eternal. And yet they are not three Eternals, but one Eternal. As there are not three Uncreated nor three Incomprehensibles, but one Uncreated and one Incomprehensible. So likewise the Father is almighty, the Son almighty, and the Holy Ghost almighty. And yet they are not three Almighties, but one Almighty.*

D. *So the Father is God, the Son is God, and the Holy Ghost is God. And yet they are not three Gods, but one God. So likewise the Father is Lord, the Son Lord, and the Holy Ghost Lord. And yet not three Lords, but one Lord. For like as we are compelled by the Christian verity to acknowledge every Person by Himself to be God and Lord, So are we forbidden by the catholic religion to say, There be three Gods, or three Lords.*

E.   *The Father is made of none: neither created nor begotten. The Son is of the Father alone; not made, nor created, but begotten. The Holy Ghost is of the Father and of the Son: neither made, nor created, nor begotten, but proceeding. So there is one Father, not three Fathers; one Son, not three Sons; one Holy Ghost, not three Holy Ghosts. And in this Trinity none is before or after other; none is greater or less than another; But the whole three Persons are coeternal together, and coequal: so that in all things, as is aforesaid, the Unity in Trinity and the Trinity in Unity is to be worshiped. He, therefore, that will be saved must thus think of the Trinity.*

F.   *Furthermore, it is necessary to everlasting salvation that he also believe faithfully the incarnation of our Lord Jesus Christ. For the right faith is, that we believe and confess that our Lord Jesus Christ, the Son of God, is God and Man; God of the Substance of the Father, begotten before the worlds; and Man of the substance of His mother, born in the world; Perfect God and perfect Man, of a reasonable soul and human flesh subsisting. Equal to the Father as touching His Godhead, and inferior to the Father as touching His manhood; Who, although He be God and Man, yet He is not two, but one Christ: One, not by conversion of the Godhead into flesh, but by taking the manhood into God; One altogether; not by confusion of Substance, but by unity of Person.*

G.   *For as the reasonable soul and flesh is one man, so God and Man is one Christ; Who suffered for our salvation; descended into hell, rose again the third day from the dead; He ascended into heaven; He sitteth on the right hand of the Father, God Almighty; from whence He shall come to judge the quick and the dead. At whose coming all men shall rise again with their bodies, and shall give an account of their own works. And they that have done good shall go into life everlasting; and they that have done evil, into everlasting fire. This is the catholic faith, which except a man believe faithfully, he cannot be saved.*

II.   THE DOCTRINE OF THE TRINITY IN SCRIPTURE

A.   The term "Trinity" is not found in the Word of God, but it speaks of the unity in the Godhead (the Father, Son and Holy Spirit). In the Godhead, there are three distinct Persons, but there is only one God.

*And Jesus came and spoke to them, saying, "All authority has been given to Me in heaven and on earth. Go therefore and make disciples of all the nations, baptizing them **in the name of the Father and of the Son and of the Holy Spirit** . . ." (Matthew 28:18–19, emphasis added)*

B.   Scripture clearly indicates that the Son and the Spirit being two distinct Persons who are both God.

    1.   The Son is God.

        a. John 1:1–3,14

        b. John 5:17,21,26

        c. John 8:58

        d. John 14:7

        e. John 20:28

        f. Revelation 1:11,17

    2.   The Spirit is God.

        a. Matthew 12:31

        b. Luke 1:35

        c. John 14:16–17

        d. John 16:7–15

        e. 2 Corinthians 3:17

        f. 2 Corinthians 13:14

        g. Ephesians 4:4–6

        h. 1 Peter 1:2–3

        i. Revelation 1:4

III.   THE MYSTERY OF THE TRINITY

A.   The reality of the Trinity is one that must be entered into through meditation where worship becomes the conduit and container for revelation and understanding.

B.   Because of the mystery of the Trinity, many have dismissed the doctrine of the Trinity as true but impractical. As a result, the Trinity has been trivialized, fallen into the background of our communion with God, and is considered irrelevant to our day-to-day living.

C.   I believe that there is significant impact that awaits us when our communion becomes Trinitarian, because Trinitarian thinking and communion causes us to get our eyes off of ourselves and get lost in the divine fellowship into which we have been called.

D.   *The modern culture of subjectivity has long since been in danger of turning into a culture of narcissism, which makes the self its own prisoner and supplies it merely with self-repetitions and self-confirmations. It is therefore time for Christian theology to break out of this prison of narcissism, and for it to present its doctrine of faith as one of the all-embracing history of God. This does not mean falling back into objectivistic orthodoxy. What it does mean is that experience of the self has to be integrated into the experience of God, and the experience of God has to be integrated into the Trinitarian history of God with the world. God is no longer related to the narrow limits of a forgiven, individual self. On the contrary, the individual self will be discovered in the overriding history of God and only finds its meaning in that context.*[1]

And now, O Father, glorify Me together with Yourself, with the glory which I had with You before the world was. (John 17:5)

And the glory which You gave Me I have given them, that they may be one just as We are one . . . (John 17:22)

*God is faithful, by whom you were called into **the fellowship of His Son**, Jesus Christ our Lord. (1 Corinthians 1:9, emphasis added)*

*The **grace of the Lord Jesus Christ**, and **the love of God**, and **the communion of the Holy Spirit** be with you all. Amen. (2 Corinthians 13:14, emphasis added)*

---

1   Jurgen Moltmann. *The Trinity and the Kingdom* (Minneapolis: First Fortress Press, 1993), p. 5.

E.   The reality of the Trinity is to be primarily encountered and secondarily grasped.

1.   *Every man lives by faith, the nonbeliever as well as the saint; the one by faith in natural laws and the other by faith in God. Every man throughout his entire life constantly accepts without understanding.*[2]

F.   *In several European languages, understanding a thing means 'grasping' it. We grasp a thing when 'we've got it'. If we have grasped something, we take it into our possession. If we possess something we can do with it what we want.*[3]

G.   *For the Greek philosophers and the Fathers of the church, knowing meant something different. It meant knowing in wonder. By knowing or perceiving one participates in the life of the other. Here knowing does not transform the counterpart into the property of the knower; the knower does not appropriate what he knows. On the contrary, he is transformed through sympathy, becoming a participator in what he perceives. Knowledge confers fellowship. That is why knowing, perception, only goes as far as love, sympathy and participation reach.*[4]

H.   *Where the theological perception of God and his history is concerned, there will be a modern discovery of Trinitarian thinking when there is at the same time a fundamental change in reason—a change from lordship to fellowship, from conquest to participation, from production to receptivity.*[5]

I.   Understanding is for the purpose of intimacy. The subject of the knowledge of God is not primarily to be grasped, but it is to be encountered. The reality of the Trinity has powerful contemplative value.

Thus says the LORD: *"Let not the wise man glory in his wisdom, let not the mighty man glory in his might, nor let the rich man glory in his riches; but let him who glories glory in this,* **that he understands and knows Me***, that I am the* LORD*, exercising loving-kindness, judgment, and righteousness in the earth. For in these I delight," says the* LORD. *(Jeremiah 9:23–24, emphasis added)*

---

2   Tozer, A.W. *The Knowledge of the Holy* (San Francisco: HarperSanFrancisco, 1961), p. 17.
3   Jurgen Moltmann. *The Trinity and the Kingdom* (Minneapolis: First Fortress Press, 1993), p. 9.
4   Ibid.
5   Ibid.

IV.   HOLY TRINITY—THE FULLNESS OF THE REVELATION OF GOD

A.   God is three in one, trinity in unity, three distinct Persons without confusion and yet of one substance. When God reveals Himself, it is the Trinity that is revealed to us and in us.

*The **grace of the Lord Jesus Christ**, and **the love of God**, and **the communion of the Holy Spirit** be with you all. Amen. (2 Corinthians 13:14, emphasis added)*

*But God has revealed them to us through His Spirit. For the Spirit searches all things, yes, the deep things of God. For what man knows the things of a man except the spirit of the man which is in him? Even so no one knows the things of God except the Spirit of God. **Now we have received, not the spirit of the world, but the Spirit who is from God, that we might know the things that have been freely given to us by God.** These things we also speak, not in words which man's wisdom teaches but which the **Holy Spirit teaches, comparing spiritual things with spiritual.** But the natural man does not receive **the things of the Spirit of God, for they are foolishness to him**; nor can he know them, because **they are spiritually discerned.** But he who is spiritual judges all things, yet he himself is rightly judged by no one. For "who has known the mind of the LORD that he may instruct Him?" **But we have the mind of Christ.** (1 Corinthians 2:10–16, emphasis added)*

B.   *Some persons who reject they cannot explain have denied that God is a Trinity. Subjecting the Most High to their cold, level-eyed scrutiny, they conclude that it is impossible that He could be both One and Three. **These forget that their whole life is enshrouded in mystery.**[6]*

C.   To set our minds on God is Trinitarian in reality because God is a Trinity. We do not encounter the Father apart from the Son (John 14:6) or the Son apart from the Father (John 6:44). The Godhead is encountered and revealed through the Spirit (1 Corinthians 2:10, 12).

*Finally, brethren, whatever things are **true**, whatever things are noble, whatever things are **just**, whatever things are **pure**, whatever things are **lovely**, whatever things are of **good report**, if there is any **virtue** and if there is anything **praiseworthy—meditate on these things.** (Philippians 4:8, emphasis added)*

---

6   Tozer, A.W. *The Knowledge of the Holy* (San Francisco: HarperSanFrancisco, 1961), p. 17. Emphasis added.

> *If then you were raised with Christ, seek those things which are above, where Christ is, sitting at the right hand of God. **Set your mind on things above**, not on things on the earth. (Colossians 3:1–2, emphasis added)*

V.   FAITH PLEASES GOD—INTIMACY IS THE CONDUIT FOR REVELATION

A.   *What God declares, the believing heart confesses without the need of further proof. Indeed, to seek proof is to admit doubt, and to obtain proof is to render faith superfluous. Everyone who possesses the gift of faith will recognize the wisdom of those daring words of one of the early Church fathers: "I believe that Christ died for me because it is incredible; I believe that He rose from the dead because it is impossible."*[7]

> *But without faith it is impossible to please Him, **for he who comes to God must believe that He is**, and that He is a rewarder of those who diligently seek Him. (Hebrews 11:6, emphasis added)*

B.   The reality of the Trinity is one that must be entered into through mediation where worship becomes the conduit and container for revelation and understanding.

C.   The reality of the Trinity is to be primarily encountered and secondarily grasped.

> *Every man lives by faith, the nonbeliever as well as the saint; the one by faith in natural laws and the other by faith in God. Every man throughout his entire life constantly accepts without understanding.*[8]

> *In several European languages, understanding a thing means 'grasping' it. We grasp as thing when 'we've got it'. If we have grasped something, we take it into our possession. If we possess something we can do with it what we want.*[9]

---

7   Tozer, A.W. *The Knowledge of the Holy* (San Francisco: HarperSanFrancisco, 1961), p. 19.
8   Ibid., p. 17.
9   Jurgen, Moltmann. *The Trinity and the Kingdom* (Minneapolis: First Fortress Press, 1993), p. 9.

D. *For the Greek philosophers and the Fathers of the church, knowing meant something different. It meant knowing in wonder. By knowing or perceiving one participates in the life of the other. Here knowing does not transform the counterpart into the property of the knower; the knower does not appropriate what he knows. On the contrary, he is transformed through sympathy, becoming a participator in what he perceives. Knowledge confers fellowship. That is why knowing, perception, only goes as far as love, sympathy and participation reach.[10]*

　　1. *. . . Faith must precede all effort to understand. Reflection upon revealed truth naturally follows the advent of faith, but faith comes first to the hearing ear, not to the cogitating mind. The believing man does not ponder the Word and arrive at faith by a process of reasoning, not does he seek confirmation of faith from philosophy or science.[11]*

E. We are to peer into the mystery of the Trinity with the eyes of our understanding enlightened by the light of the Holy Spirit. This is a reality that we encounter with our spirit through mediation on the written Word of God.

　　*The **grace of the Lord Jesus Christ**, and the **love of God**, and the **communion of the Holy Spirit** be with you all. Amen. (2 Corinthians 13:14, emphasis added)*

F. A.W. Tozer states: "Love and faith are at home in the mystery of the Godhead."[12]

VI.　THE NECESSITY OF RECOVERING TRINITARIAN THINKING

A. The mystery of the Trinity has been trivialized as an intellectual aspect of theology. Yet the doctrine of the Trinity is primarily about worship, not academic thinking. The shroud of mystery surrounding the Trinity should powerfully exhilarate our hearts with fascination and worship. This doctrine must be rediscovered, pulled off the shelves of intellectualism and brought back to its rightful place in liturgy and devotion. The mystery of the Trinity needs to be the focal point of contemplation, communion, and the adoring gaze of the Body of Christ Jesus once again.

10　Ibid.
11　Tozer, A.W. *The Knowledge of the Holy* (San Francisco: HarperSanFrancisco, 1961), p. 19.
12　Ibid., p. 20.

B.   Throughout Church history, the doctrine of the Trinity became more and more linked with stale intellectualism with a new move toward and emphasis on "subjectivism." During the time of Friedrich Schleiermacher, this doctrine slowly started to be viewed as truth, but not a relevant truth as it relates to every believer's encounters with God. Schleiermacher brought the reality of feeling God back to the Church's attention.

C.   The doctrine of the Trinity was pushed aside because it was seen as impractical. It is my opinion that this is a great error because the knowledge of God is Trinitarian. The Trinity is who and what God is. When Christ reveals God by the Spirit of God, He reveals to us the eternal fellowship of the Godhead. When God reveals God, He reveals the Father, the Son, and the Spirit.

D.   Returning to Trinitarian thinking is not only vital, but it is the very longing of Christ to usher us into His fellowship. To be swallowed in the Trinity is our inheritance.

God is faithful, by whom you were called into the fellowship of His Son, Jesus Christ our Lord. (1 Corinthians 1:9)

*If anyone loves Me, he will keep My word; and My Father will love him, and **We** will come to him and make **Our home** with him. He who does not love Me does not keep My words; and the word which you hear is not Mine but the Father's who sent Me. These things I have spoken to you while being present with you. **But the Helper, the Holy Spirit, whom the Father will send in My name, He will teach you all things, and bring to your remembrance all things that I said to you.** (John 14:23–26, emphasis added)*

*And now, O Father, glorify Me together with Yourself, **with the glory which I had with You before the world was.** (John 17:5, emphasis added)*

*And **the glory which You gave Me I have given them**, that they may be one just as We are one. (John 17:22, emphasis added)*

But God has revealed them to us through His Spirit. For the Spirit searches all things, yes, the deep things of God. For what man knows the things of a man except the spirit of the man which is in him? Even so no one knows the things of God except the Spirit of God. Now we have received, not the spirit of the world, but the Spirit who is from God, that we might know the things that have been freely given to us by God. (1 Corinthians 2:10–12, emphasis added)

E.   True community is profoundly rooted in Trinitarian reality and contemplation.

. . . That they all may be one, as You, Father, are in Me, and I in You; that they also may be one in Us, that the world may believe that You sent Me. And *the glory which You gave Me I have given them, that they may be one just as We are one: I in them, and You in Me; that they may be made perfect in one,* and that the world may know that You have sent Me, and have loved them as You have loved Me. (John 17:21–23, emphasis added)

. . . That which we have seen and heard we declare to you, that you also may have fellowship with us; and truly our fellowship is with the Father and with His Son Jesus Christ. (1 John 1:3, emphasis added)

VII.   THE TRINITY AND THE ETERNAL MYSTERY (EPHESIANS CHAPTERS 1–3)

A.   In the holy counsel of the Trinity, the Father is the author and initiator of the mystery.

1.   He dispenses grace (1:2) and blesses with spiritual blessings (1:3).

2.   He chose us in Christ (1:4), He predestined us (1:5), and He made us accepted (1:6).

3.   The mystery of the Father's will is revealed (1:9)—the gathering of Heaven and Earth (1:10; Psalm 119:96).

4.   He works all things according to the counsel of His will (1:11).

5.   He is identified as the Father of glory (1:17).

6.   The hope of His calling can be known (1:18).

7.   His inheritance is in the saints (1:18, 1:22–23, 1 Corinthians 15).

8.   He demonstrates the power by which He raised Christ from the dead and ascended Jesus to the highest place in the New Jerusalem (1:3, 20–21).

9.   He put all things under Jesus' feet and appointed Christ as leader over all.

10.   He called the Church to be the fullness of God's expression, personality and purpose (Genesis 1:26; Ephesians 3:10).

11.   He is rich in mercy and filled with great love (2:4).

12.   He made us alive (2:5).

13.   He raised us up to be seated in heavenly places (2:6, 1:3).

14.   He is filled with exceeding riches of grace and kindness (2:7).

15.   He gives salvation (2:8).

16.   He is the giver, the revealer, of the mystery (3:3).

17.   He is the giver of the promise (3:6).

B.   The Son, under the leadership of the Father, administrates the mystery of God.

1.   He dispenses grace and peace (1:2).

2.   Jesus is the Son of God (1:3, 1:17).

3.   He gives us the right to be sons of God (1:5; John 1:12).

4.   He is the Beloved (1:6).

5.   He is the redeemer (1:7).

6.   The fullness of God is revealed in Him (1:10).

7.   He was raised from the dead and ascended on high (1:20–21).

8.   He is the head of the Church (1:22–23).

9.   We are seated in heavenly places in Him (2:6).

10.   He is the One in whom the kindness of the Father is revealed (2:7).

11.   Through Christ we can accomplish the will of God (2:10).

12.   He is the One who brought us near (1:4, 2:6, 2:13).

13.   He abolished enmity. He is our peace (2:15; Romans 5:1).

14.   He is the creator of the New Man (Jew and Gentile Romans 9:23–24).

15.   He reconciled Jew and Gentile to God (2:16).

16.   He grants us access to the Father (2:6, 2:17).

17.   He is the Chief cornerstone (Psalm 118:22).

18.   He is the temple of God (2:20–22, Revelation 21:22).

19.   Creation was made through Him (3:10).

20.   The plan of God is accomplished in Christ (3:11).

C.   Under the leadership of the Father and the Son, the Holy Spirit executes the plans of the Father.

1.   He is the seal of God and the guarantee of our inheritance (1:13–14).

2.   He is the Spirit of wisdom and revelation (1:17).

3.   He is our divine escort to the Father (2:18).

4.   He takes residence in the people of God (2:22).

5.   He reveals the mystery (3:5; John 14, 16).

6.   He is the Spirit of might (3:16).

Session Nine: The Fullness of the Godhead Revealed in Christ Jesus

I. **THE BRANCH OF THE LORD WILL BE SHOWN FORTH BEAUTIFUL AND GLORIOUS**

In that day the Branch of the LORD shall be beautiful and glorious . . . (Isaiah 4:2)

A. The Father's zeal is to put His Son on display at the end of the age. The Holy Spirit is going to release a fresh revelation of who Jesus is to the Church. This revelation is the **foundation** of the Church.

*Jesus answered and said to him, "Blessed are you, Simon Bar-Jonah, **for flesh and blood has not revealed this to you**, but My Father who is in heaven. And I also say to you that you are Peter, and **on this rock I will build My church** . . ." (Matthew 16:17–18, emphasis added)*

*For no other **foundation** can anyone lay than that which is laid, which is **Jesus Christ.** (1 Corinthians 3:11, emphasis added)*

B. The Father has great passion and delight in revealing His Son.

Behold! My Servant . . . in whom My soul delights. (Isaiah 42:1)

Jesus dwells in the embrace of God the Father forever. The power of the Father's delight is so strong that Jesus desires the Father to impart His heart for the Son in the Bride of Christ Jesus.

And I have declared to them Your name, and will declare it, that the love with which You loved Me may be in them, and I in them. (John 17:26)

No one has seen God at any time. The only begotten Son, who is in the bosom of the Father, He has declared Him. (John 1:18)

II. **CHRIST IS GOD'S FINAL WORD TO HUMANITY**

God, who at various times and in various ways spoke in time past to the fathers by the prophets, has in these last days spoken to us by His Son, whom He has appointed heir of all things, through whom also He made the worlds; who being the brightness of His glory and the express image of His person, and upholding all things by the word of His power, when He had by Himself purged our sins, sat down at the right hand of the Majesty on high . . . (Hebrews 1:1–3)

A.   God speaks in many various ways, indicating His longing to make Himself known to humanity. God speaks for the first time in Genesis 1, declaring, "Let there be light." It is my opinion that the first in-breaking of light is the revelation of His glory in the face of Christ (2 Corinthians 4:6). I refer to Genesis 1 as the vision statement of the Father's desire to see all of created order filled with the knowledge of His glory.

B.   The revelation of God through the prophets was partial and merely whispers compared to the thunder of the fullness of revelation that came through the Son of God. God spoke His final and decisive decree in and through Christ. All that God has to say about Himself is proclaimed in and through the Person of Christ. Christ is God's decisive word to humanity. The revelation of the knowledge of God is found only in Jesus.

In the beginning was the Word, and the Word was with God, and the Word was God. He was in the beginning with God. All things were made through Him, and without him nothing was made that has been made . . . And the Word became flesh and dwelt among us and we beheld His glory, the glory of the only begotten of the Father, full of grace and truth. (John 1:1–3,14)

*No one has seen God at any time. The only begotten Son, **who is in the bosom of the Father**, He has declared Him. (John 1:18, emphasis added)*

*Jesus said to him, "Have I been with you so long, and yet you have not known Me, Philip? **He who has seen Me has seen the Father**; so how can you say, 'Show us the Father?'" (John 14:9, emphasis added)*

***He is the image of the invisible God**, the firstborn over all creation. For by Him all things were created that are in heaven and that are on earth, visible and invisible, whether thrones or dominions or principalities or powers. All things were created through Him and for Him. **And He is before all things, and in Him all things consist.** (Colossians 1:15–17, emphasis added)*

***For in Him dwells all the fullness of the Godhead bodily**; and you are complete in Him, who is the head of all principality and power. (Colossians 2:9–10, emphasis added)*

III.   THE SEVENFOLD BEAUTY OF GOD REVEALED IN CHRIST (HEBREWS 1:1–3)

A.   **Number one: God appointed Him heir over all things** (displaying the Kingship of Christ). Christ is God's chosen King to rule and reign over the kingdoms of this world. Jesus will establish God's theocratic government on the earth. In the end, the kingdoms of this world will become the kingdoms of the Lord and His Christ (Isaiah 42:1–4; 1 Corinthians 15:25–28; Revelation 5:1–10, 11:15–19).

*I was watching in the night visions, and **behold, One like the Son of Man**, coming with the clouds of heaven! He came to the Ancient of Days, and they brought Him near before Him. **Then to Him was given dominion and glory and a kingdom, that all peoples, nations, and languages should serve Him.** His dominion is an everlasting dominion, which shall not pass away, and His kingdom the one which shall not be destroyed. (Daniel 7:13–14, emphasis added)*

1.   The exaltation of Christ glorifies the Father. There are many things revealed about the character of God in the exaltation of Christ.

. . . And that every tongue should confess that Jesus Christ is Lord, to the glory of God the Father. (Philippians 2:11)

B.   **Number two: It was through Him that God made the universe.** Everything that was made came about through the Father's creative decree. Jesus is the decree of the Father. He is the Word (Logos) of God. Jesus is called the **Word that was with God and that is God** (John 1:1). Jesus, the living intercessory oracle, manifested His power in **Genesis 1.** He revealed the Father's desire in declaring the Father's decrees by both creating and then sustaining (governing) everything under the Father.

1.   *The Logos was one of the most important elements in Stoic theology. The Stoics used the idea of the Logos to provide the basis for a rational moral life. Face with the usual Greek dualism of God and the world, they employed the concept of Logos as a unitary idea to solve the problem of duality. The entire universe was conceived as forming a single living whole that was permeated in all its parts by a primitive power conceived a never-resting, all pervading fire or fiery vapor. The precise character of this essential fire is not clear; writers differ in their understanding of it. It was a diffused, tenuous kind of fiery air, possessing property of thought. This very refined substance was thought to be immanent in all the world and to appear in living beings as the soul. It is a divine world-power, containing within itself the conditions and processes of all things, and is called Logos or God. As a productive power, the divine Logos was called the spermatikos logos, the Seminal Logos or generative principle of the world. This vital energy both pervades the universe and unfolds itself into innumerable logoi spermatikoi or formative forces that energize the manifold phenomena of nature and life. This Logos, by pervading all things, provides the rational order of the universe and supplies the standard for conduct and for the proper ordering of life for the rational person. The rational individual is the one who lives in accordance with nature, and thereby finds an all-determining law of conduct.*[1]

2.   Everything created is for and through the Son of God (Proverbs 8:22–31).

     You are worthy, O Lord, to receive glory and honor and power; **for You created all things, and by Your will they exist and were created.** *(Revelation 4:11, emphasis added)*

---

1   Ladd, George Eldon. *A Theology of the New Testament.* (Grand Rapids: Wm. B. Eerdmans Publishing Company), p. 275.

> The LORD possessed me at the beginning of His way, before His works of old. I have been established from everlasting, from the beginning, before there was ever an earth. When there were no depths I was brought forth, when there were no fountains abounding with water. Before the mountains were settled, before the hills, I was brought forth; While as yet He had not made the earth or the fields, or the primal dust of the world. When He prepared the heavens, I was there, when He drew a circle on the face of the deep, when He established the clouds above, when He strengthened the fountains of the deep, when He assigned to the sea its limit, so that the waters would not transgress His command, when He marked out the foundations of the earth, then I was beside Him as a master craftsman; and I was daily His delight, rejoicing always before Him, rejoicing in His inhabited world, and my delight was with the sons of men. (Proverbs 8:22–31)

3. *The word of God was an important concept to the Jew; creation came into being and was preserved by the word of God (Gen 1:3, "and God said"; see Ps 33:6, 9; 47:15–18); and the word of God is the bearer of salvation and new life (Ps 107:20; Isa 4:8; Ezek 37:4–5). In the Old Testament, the word is not merely an utterance; it is a semi-hypostatized existence so that it can go forth and accomplish the divine purpose (Isa 55:10–11). The word of God uttered at creation, expressed through the mouth of the prophets (cf. Jer 1:4, 11; 2:1) and in the Law (Ps 119:38, 41, 105), has a number of functions that may very well be compared with those attributed to the Logos in John. The concept of personified wisdom also provides Jewish background for the Logos concept.*[2]

C. **Number three: He is the effulgence or the radiance of God's glory.** Christ is the glory of God, meaning that the very character and nature of God's personality is revealed in Him and through Him.

1. Revelation of God is revealed in the face of Christ. The radiance is the revelation of God. Jesus is God revealing God to humanity (2 Corinthians 4:6). Jesus is the light of the world (John 8:12) and He is also the source of revelation inside of us (Colossians 1:27).

---

2   Ladd, George Eldon. *A Theology of the New Testament.* (Grand Rapids: Wm. B. Eerdmans Publishing Company, 1974), p. 276.

D.   **Number four: He is the very image of the essence of God.**

Jesus is the shining of God's glory among men. He says that he was the charactēr *of God's very essence. In Greek,* charactēr *means two things: first, a seal, and, second, the impression that the seal leaves on the wax. The impression has the exact form of the seal. So, when the writer to the Hebrews said that Jesus was the* charactēr *of the being of God, He meant that he was the exact image of God. Just as when you look at the impression, you see exactly what the seal which made it is like, so when you look at Jesus you see exactly what God is like.*[3]

1.   The very nature of the character of God is stamped upon the nature and essence of Christ. Just as the glory of God is reflected, so the being of God is truly in Christ. It pleased the Father that the fullness should dwell in Him (Colossians 1:19, 2:9).

E.   **Number five: He upholds all things by the word of His power.**

1.   Jesus is the intercessory oracle of God by which all that is created is sustained. It is God's same creative power that now sustains all things. Christ is the sustainer and governor of God's created order.

2.   Jesus sustains, upholds or holds together, the created order **by speaking** the Word (type of intercession) to the Father **in the present tense.**

*And Jesus came and spoke to them, saying, "**All authority has been given to Me in heaven and on earth.** Go therefore and make disciples of all the nations, baptizing them in the name of the Father and of the Son and of the Holy Spirit . . ." (Matthew 28:18–19, emphasis added)*

*And He is before all things, and **in Him all things consist.** (Colossians 1:17, emphasis added)*

3.   Job 38–41 shows us the beauty of God's sustaining power over all creation.

---

3   Barclay, William. *The Letter to the Hebrews*. The Daily Study Bible series, rev. ed. (The Westminster Press: Philadelphia, 2000, c. 1975), as quoted in *Scholar's Library: Silver* (Logos Bible Software: 2004). Emphasis added.

F. **Number six: He has made purification for our sins.**

1. The first four realities connect us with the eternity and transcendence of God. However, now we see that the transcendent God became an eminent and intimate reality when He became a Man and pursued us even unto death. The transcendent God came into the world and dwelt among us to function as a High Priest and offer Himself as the sacrifice for our sins.

2. He offered Himself—transcendent majesty became the sacrifice for our sins that we might enter into His eternal dwellings. I believe this reality is the central theme of the book of Hebrews.

3. Jesus' sacrifice impacts the human spirit in two different yet basic ways. The transcendence of Christ produces wonder and fascination in our spirit, while the eminence produces a sense of intimacy, fulfillment and gratitude.

G. **Number seven: He sat down at the right hand of the majesty on high.**

1. The ascension of Christ fills all in all (Psalm 110).

2. Exaltation, supremacy and preeminence are His.

   A. *. . . Ascended far above all the heavens that he might fill all things. (Ephesians 4:10)*

IV. **THE TENFOLD BEAUTY OF JESUS (SONG 5:11–16)**

*His **head** is like the finest gold; His **locks** are wavy . . . His **eyes** are like doves . . . His **cheeks** are like a bed of spices . . . His **lips** are lilies . . . His **hands** are rods of gold . . . His **body** is carved ivory . . . His **legs** are pillars of marble . . . His **countenance** is like Lebanon . . . His **mouth** is most sweet, yes, **He is altogether lovely**. This is my Beloved, and this is my friend . . . (Song 5:11–16, emphasis added)*

*Jesus said to him, "Have I been with you so long, and yet you have not known Me, Philip? **He who has seen Me has seen the Father;** so how can you say, 'Show us the Father'?" (John 14:9, emphasis added)*

A.   The Song of Solomon is an allegorical book inspired by the Holy Spirit to depict holy natural, married love and also to give spiritual insight into the holy romance of the Gospel between the Bridegroom God and the Bride of Christ.

B.   Allegorical interpretations are helpful if we only use them to illustrate truths that are clearly established throughout the New Testament. In Song 5:10–16 there is a powerful description of the tenfold beauty of Christ.

   1.   His head—His perfect leadership

   2.   His locks—His zeal for the Father and for His Bride

   3.   His eyes—His omniscience

   4.   His cheeks—His emotions (the deep things of God)

   5.   His lips—His word

   6.   His hands—His administration

   7.   His body—His tender compassion

   8.   His legs—the execution of His divine administration and purpose

   9.   His countenance—the impartation of the knowledge of God to His people (2 Corinthians 4:6)

   10.   His mouth—intimacy with Him

V.   THE KNOWLEDGE OF GOD IN THE APOCALYPSE OF CHRIST

The Revelation of Jesus Christ, which God gave Him to show His servants— things which must shortly take place. And He sent and signified it by His angel to His servant John, who bore witness to the word of God, and to the testimony of Jesus Christ, to all things that he saw. Blessed is he who reads and those who hear the words of this prophecy, and keep those things which are written in it; for the time is near. (Revelation 1:1–3, emphasis added)

A.   The Revelation (Apocalypse) of Christ, given by the Father, contains information concerning things that must shortly take place. The events highlighted in this book are meant to give the end-time church insight into the knowledge of God revealed in Christ. The **end-time wonders** released are meant to give understanding.

*Our fathers in Egypt did not **understand Your wonders**; They did not remember the multitude of Your mercies, but rebelled by the sea—the Red Sea. (Psalm 106:7, emphasis added)*

B. The Revelation of Christ speaks of the fierceness of His leadership, culminating with the events of the Second Coming as He leads the earth into the fullness of that which He accomplished through His death, burial and resurrection.

> *For it pleased the Father that in Him all the fullness should dwell, and by Him* **to reconcile all things to Himself, by Him, whether things on earth or things in heaven,** *having made peace* **through the blood of His cross.** *(Colossians 1:19–20, emphasis added)*

C. This great end-time book is about both the unveiling of events and the beauty of the person of Christ Jesus. Somehow Jesus' divine administrations are powerfully and intricately woven together with revelation of His beauty. John received the revelation by an angelic messenger who was dispatched by the Son of God under the leadership and the decree of the Father.

D. As the administration and the personhood of Christ are revealed, so is the beauty and the glory of God the Father. The book of Revelation shows us God's sovereignty over human history. The Father is seen as the master architect behind the blueprint of the ages—the mystery of His will (Ephesians 1:9). Christ executes the Father's master plan (Revelation 10:7).

> *Jesus said to him, "Have I been with you so long, and yet you have not known Me, Philip?* **He who has seen Me has seen the Father;** *so how can you say, 'Show us the Father'? Do you not believe that I am in the Father, and the Father in Me?* **The words that I speak to you I do not speak on My own authority; but the Father who dwells in Me does the work** *(including the administration seen in the book of Revelation)…"* *(John 14:9–10, emphasis and parenthetical comment added)*

> *. . .* **Who** *(Jesus)* **being the brightness of His glory** *(the Father)* **and the express image of His person** *(the Father), and upholding all things by the word of His power, when He had by Himself purged our sins, sat down at the right hand of the Majesty on high . . . (Hebrews 1:3, emphasis and parenthetical comments added)*

E. The book of Revelation is Jesus continuing to declare the name of the Father in order to awaken love in the heart of the end-time Church (John 17:26). The content of the book is meant to fuel and energize an adoring gaze of worship and prayer. The unveiling of the mystery of God and the testimony of Jesus, read with a devotional spirit, produces the response seen in Revelation 19:10.

> *And **I fell at his feet to worship him.** But he said to me, "See that you do not do that! I am your fellow servant, and of your brethren who have the testimony of Jesus. **Worship God!** For the testimony* (heart) *of Jesus is the spirit of prophecy." (Revelation 19:10, emphasis and parenthetical comment added)*

F.   The book of Revelation is as much about the Son revealing the Father as it is the Father revealing the Son. 1:1 says that God gave the revelation to the Son who sent the angel.

G.   There is, therefore, no need to debate over who the sole revealer is, whether the Father or the Son. We can see the Father's desire for His Son, using all the resources of Heaven to vindicate and glorify Him. We also see the Father's desire to see the Bride of the Lamb emerge from the nations of the earth. The book of Revelation is the Father showing Himself strong on Christ's behalf, causing all of natural history to be summed up in Christ, who is the consummation of all perfection.

> *And **I have declared to them Your name, and will declare it,** that the love with which You loved Me may be in them, and I in them. (John 17:26, emphasis added)*

> *I have seen **the consummation of all perfection** (Christ Jesus), but Your commandment is exceedingly broad. (Psalm 119:96, emphasis and parenthetical comment added)*

VI.   THE GLORY OF THE SON OF MAN (REVELATION 1:13–17)

A.   **One like the Son of Man (1:13a):** Jesus is seen as One in the midst of the seven lampstands. Jesus is not only the transcendent Son of God, but He is also the Son of Man who is near His people and in their midst.

B.   **Clothed with a garment down to the feet and girded about the chest with a golden band (1:13b):** The Son of Man was clothed with a garment down to His feet, which speaks of His priestly office and ministry before God and amongst the Church. The writer of Hebrews calls Jesus our Apostle and High Priest who was more worthy than Moses (Hebrews 3:1).

> *Therefore, holy brethren, partakers of the heavenly calling, **consider the Apostle and High Priest of our confession, Christ Jesus,** who was faithful to Him who appointed Him, as Moses also was faithful in all His house. For this One has been counted worthy of more glory than Moses, inasmuch as He who built the house has more honor than the house. For every house is built by someone, but He who built all things is God. (Hebrews 3:1–4, emphasis added)*

1. Christ is the Apostle in that He is God's messenger and representative; He is also the High Priest, our representative before God. Jesus' garments speak of His priestly ministry on our behalf in that the High Priest was appointed for men.

2. In the book of Hebrews, the first mention of Jesus' priestly ministry is in the context of His ability to sympathize with a suffering Church and her temptation to draw back. Christ, our High Priest, is sympathetic toward us in our weakness and intercedes for us. He was tempted in every way and so is able to sympathize in His humanity and help the suffering Church at the end of the age through His leadership and intercession. This revelation of Christ the sympathetic High Priest will fuel the Church at the end of the age with boldness to draw near to Him in prayer even while under pressure.

    > *Therefore, in all things He had to be made like His brethren, **that He might be a merciful and faithful High Priest in things pertaining to God,** to make propitiation for the sins of the people. **For in that He Himself has suffered, being tempted, He is able to aid those who are tempted** (tempted to apostatize under pressure). (Hebrews 2:17–18, emphasis and parenthetical comment added)*

3. Jesus is the High Priest in the order of Melchizedek. The priesthood of Melchizedek is unto understanding the fullness of the knowledge of God. Melchizedek brings the revelation of God as Lord, Possessor of Heaven and Earth. I believe Melchizedek ushers Abraham into a vision for fullness and the **Genesis 15:1** encounter. **Genesis 15:1** is where humanity, through Abraham, is promised the full knowledge of God, which is fulfilled in his Seed—Christ.

C. **His head and hair were white like wool, as white as snow (1:14a):** The Son of Man here has the same attributes as the Ancient of Days seen in Daniel's vision.

*I watched till thrones were put in place, and **the Ancient of Days** was seated; His garment was white as snow, and **the hair of His head was like pure wool.** His throne was a fiery flame, its wheels a burning fire . . . (Daniel 7:9, emphasis added)*

*The **silver-haired head is a crown of glory,** if it is found in the way of righteousness. (Proverbs 16:31, emphasis added)*

1.   The Son of Man stands before John as the eternal King who alone is wise. Jesus' hair that is white like wool speaks of the purity of His divine wisdom. The primary attribute of divine wisdom is purity.

   *But **the wisdom that is from above is first pure,** then peaceable, gentle, willing to yield, full of mercy and good fruits, without partiality and without hypocrisy. (James 3:17, emphasis added)*

D.   **His eyes like a flame of fire (1:14b):** According to Revelation 2:18–23, the flaming eyes could speak of Christ's ability to search the hearts and minds of His people. His eyes speak of His infinite knowledge, wisdom, understanding and discernment. The fire in His eyes reveals His zeal for the Father and His purposes in the earth.

E.   **His feet were like fine brass, as if refined in a furnace (1:15a):** Christ's feet were like fine brass as One who has stood in the place of everlasting burnings. He will administrate the judgments of the Lord. Jesus is the Apostle and High Priest who has stood in the presence of God's fire.

   . . . Who among us shall dwell with the devouring fire? Who among us shall dwell with everlasting burnings? (Isaiah 33:14)

F.   **His voice as the sound of many waters (1:15b):** This speaks of the power of Christ's voice and words. The voice of the Lord is powerful and majestic. The Father's full authority is in the voice of the Son of God.

   *The **voice of the Lord is over the waters;** the God of glory thunders; the Lord is over many waters. **The voice of the Lord is powerful;** the voice of the Lord is full of majesty. (Psalm 29:3–4, emphasis added)*

   *When they went, I heard the noise of their wings, **like the noise of many waters, like the voice of the Almighty,** a tumult like the noise of an army; and when they stood still, they let down their wings. (Ezekiel 1:24, emphasis added)*

*And they were astonished at His teaching, **for His word was with authority.** (Luke 4:32, emphasis added)*

G.   **He had in His hand seven stars (1:16a):** According to 1:20, the seven stars speak of the messengers of the churches. These stars being in the right hand of Christ indicates that these messengers are under the leadership and control of Christ Jesus. Jesus is the head of the Church.

*For the husband is head of the wife, as also **Christ is head of the church; and He is the Savior of the body.** (Ephesians 5:23, emphasis added)*

H.   **Out of His mouth went a sharp two-edged sword (1:16b):** Hebrews 4:12 calls the word of God the sword of the Spirit by which every thought and intention of the heart is discerned. The word of God is the way by which Christ wages war against God's enemies. He strikes the nations with the decrees of God as with a rod of iron. I think of Psalm 2:7–8 as that threefold divine decree:

1.   Christ is the Son of God, the begotten of the Father.

2.   It is decreed by the God the Father that Christ is to ask for the nations as His inheritance.

3.   It is the Father's decree that Christ is to rule the nations with a rod of iron and establish righteousness in the nations that the Father may come and dwell on the earth.

*I will declare the decree: The LORD has said to Me, "**You are My Son,** today I have begotten You. **Ask of Me,** and I will give You the nations for Your inheritance, and the ends of the earth for Your possession. **You shall break them with a rod of iron;** You shall dash them to pieces like a potter's vessel." (Psalm 2:7–9, emphasis added)*

I.   Christ is the One who has stood in the counsels of the Godhead and has the word of the Lord to establish the righteousness of God in the earth.

J.   In **1:17**, John falls down, overwhelmed at the sight of the splendor of Jesus. Jesus strengthens and comforts John with the revelation of eternity.

Session Ten: The Eternity of God

I.   INTRODUCTION

> *For thus says **the High and Lofty One who inhabits eternity**, whose name is **Holy: "I dwell in the high and holy place**, with him who has a contrite and humble spirit, to revive the spirit of the humble, and to revive the heart of the contrite ones." (Isaiah 57:15, emphasis added)*

A.   The subject of eternity is key to understanding the Gospel. It connects us with the big picture, in that it makes known to us God's plans and purposes as they are communicated in the Gospel. The doctrine of eternity helps us make sense of our present reality and fills us with both hope and the fear of the Lord.

B.   We should reflect often on the eternity of God and ask the Lord to grant us revelation of this reality.

C.   *The concept of everlastingness runs like a lofty mountain range throughout the entire Bible and looms large in orthodox Hebrew and Christian thought. Were we to reject the concept, it would be altogether impossible for us to think again the thoughts of the prophets and apostles . . . [1]*

D.   Eternity is the realm in which God dwells. There is no time in the realm of eternity because time is subject to measurement. There is no past, present, or future in eternity. The very name of God is **I AM.** Time dwells in God.

> *Lord, **you have been our dwelling place** throughout all generations. Before the mountains were born or you brought forth the earth and the world, **from everlasting to everlasting** you are God. You turn men back to dust, saying, "Return to dust, O sons of men." **For a thousand years in your sight are like a day that has just gone by, or like a watch in the night.** You sweep men away in the sleep of death; they are like the new grass of the morning—though in the morning it springs up new, by evening it is dry and withered. (Psalm 90:1–6, NIV, emphasis added)*

> *. . . For in Him we live and move and have our being . . . (Acts 17:28)*

E.   The doctrine of eternity gives us:

---

1   Tozer, A.W. *The Knowledge of the Holy* (San Francisco: HarperSanFrancisco, 1961), p. 38.

1.   Comfort—the duration and permanence of the promise, plans and character of God and communion with Him.

2.   Divine perspective—the big picture.

3.   Humility in the fear of the Lord—we encounter our frailty.

4.   Refuge—Acts 17:24–26.

God, who made the world and everything in it, since He is Lord of heaven and earth, does not dwell in temples made with hands. Nor is He worshiped with men's hands, as though He needed anything, since He gives to all life, breath, and all things. And He has made from one blood every nation of men to dwell on all the face of the earth, and has determined their preappointed times and the boundaries of their dwellings, so that they should seek the Lord, in the hope that they might grope for Him and find Him, though He is not far from each one of us; for in Him we live and move and have our being, as also some of your own poets have said, "For we are also His offspring." (Acts 17:24–28, emphasis added)

Lord, You have been our dwelling place in all generations. Before the mountains were brought forth, or ever You had formed the earth and the world, even from everlasting to everlasting, You are God. (Psalm 90:1–2, emphasis added)

5.   Strength in times of tribulation—Isaiah 40:28–31.

Why do you say, O Jacob, and speak, O Israel: "My way is hidden from the LORD, and my just claim is passed over by my God?" Have you not known? Have you not heard? The everlasting God, the LORD, the Creator of the ends of the earth, neither faints nor is weary. His understanding is unsearchable. He gives power to the weak, and to those who have no might He increases strength. Even the youths shall faint and be weary, and the young men shall utterly fall, but those who wait on the LORD shall renew their strength; they shall mount up with wings like eagles, they shall run and not be weary, they shall walk and not faint. (Isaiah 40:27–31, emphasis added)

6.   Wisdom to live in a place of trusting the Lord—Psalm 39:4–6.

> *LORD, make me to know my end, and what is the measure of my days, that I may know how frail I am. Indeed, You have made my days as handbreadths, and my age is as nothing before You; certainly every man at his best state is but vapor. Surely every man walks about like a shadow; surely they busy themselves in vain; he heaps up riches, and does not know who will gather them. (Psalm 39:4–6)*

F.   The revelation of eternity connects us with the reality of God. When our hearts are connected with the truth of God's eternity, it takes us out of the surreal and ushers us into the real.

II.   ETERNITY IN OUR HEARTS

A.   Our hearts are designed to yearn for eternity. Humans tremble with fascination before this mysterious subject.

> *He has made everything beautiful in its time. Also **He has put eternity in their hearts**, except that no one can find out the work that God does from beginning to end. (Ecclesiastes 3:11, emphasis added)*

B.   He has made everything beautiful **in its time.**

> *Then He who sat on the throne said, "Behold, **I make all things new.**" And He said to me, "Write, for these words are true and faithful." (Revelation 21:5, emphasis added)*

   1.   God will make all things new (beautiful) in the fullness of the dispensation of time.

   2.   God's plans will not be thwarted.

C.   He has put **eternity in our hearts.**

> ***One thing I have desired of the LORD**, that will I seek: that I may dwell in the house of the LORD all the days of my life, **to behold the beauty of the LORD**, and to inquire in His temple. (Psalm 27:4, emphasis added)*

   1.   God has put a longing and desire in humanity for the reality of eternity.

   2.   It takes the revelation of eternity to satisfy the longing of our hearts.

But God has revealed them to us through His Spirit. For the Spirit searches all things, yes, the deep things of God. For what man knows the things of a man except the spirit of the man which is in him? Even so no one knows the things of God except the Spirit of God. Now we have received, not the spirit of the world, but the Spirit who is from God, that we might know the things that have been freely given to us by God. (1 Corinthians 2:10–12)

D.   Yet **no one can find out the work** that God does from beginning to end.

*But we **speak the wisdom of God in a mystery**, the hidden wisdom which God **ordained before the ages for our glory** . . . (1 Corinthians 2:7, emphasis added)*

*Now **we have received**, not the spirit of the world, but **the Spirit who is from God**, that we might know the **things that have been freely given to us by God. These things** we also speak, not in words which man's wisdom teaches but which the Holy Spirit teaches, **comparing spiritual things with spiritual**. But the natural man does not receive the things of the Spirit of God, for they are foolishness to him; nor can he know them, **because they are spiritually discerned.** (1 Corinthians 2:12–14, emphasis added)*

Oh, the depth of the riches both of the wisdom and knowledge of God! How unsearchable are His judgments and His ways past finding out! *"For **who has known the mind** of the L*ORD*? Or who has become His counselor? Or who has first given to Him and it shall be repaid to him?" For **of Him** and **through Him** and **to Him** are all things, to whom be glory forever. Amen. (Romans 11:33–36, emphasis added)*

1.   Though there is deep longing in the human heart for eternity, we cannot make sense of it apart from the spirit of revelation touching our hearts because it is the mystery of the eternal Gospel of God.

2.   God longs to fill the depths of our being with the deep things of His heart.

*For this reason we also, since the day we heard it, do not cease to pray for you, and to ask that you may **be filled with the knowledge of His will** in all wisdom and spiritual understanding. (Colossians 1:9, emphasis added)*

*To them God willed to make known what are the riches of the glory of this mystery among the Gentiles; which is **Christ in you the hope of glory.** (Colossians 1:27, emphasis added)*

III.   THE DOCTRINE OF ETERNITY AND THE FRAILTY OF LIFE

So teach us to number our days, that we may gain a heart of wisdom. (Psalm 90:12)

A.   The revelation of eternity confronts us with the brevity of life and the fear of the Lord. Eternity puts the **finitude of humanity** and our frame face to face with the **infinitude of God.**

B.   The mystery of infinitude is that God has always been and will always be. The eternity of God refers to the reality that He existed before the foundations of the earth and that He will continue and endure forever, throughout all eternity future.

*Holy, holy, holy, Lord God Almighty, **Who was and is and is to come!** (Revelation 4:8, emphasis added)*

*"I am the **Alpha and the Omega, the Beginning and the End,"** says the Lord, "who is and who was and who is to come, the Almighty." (Revelation 1:8, emphasis added)*

*. . . Saying, "I am the **Alpha and the Omega, the First and the Last . . .**" (Revelation 1:11, emphasis added)*

*And when I saw Him, I fell at His feet as dead. But He laid His right hand on me, saying to me, "Do not be afraid; **I am the First and the Last.**" (Revelation 1:17, emphasis added)*

*. . . Looking unto Jesus, **the author and finisher of our faith,** who for the joy that was set before Him endured the cross, despising the shame, and has sat down at the right hand of the throne of God. (Hebrews 12:2, emphasis added)*

C.   *If we would look back, we can reach no further than the beginning of the creation, and account the years from the first foundation of the world; but after that we must lose ourselves in the abyss of eternity; we have no cue to guide our thoughts; we can see no bounds in thy eternity.*[2]

---

2   Charnock, Stephen. *The Existence and Attributes of God, Volume One* (Grand Rapids: Baker Books, 2005), p. 278.

D.   The eternity of God is attributed to the reality that He as always been, will always be, has none before Him nor after Him. God is—hence the name I AM. The eternity of God speaks of constancy in that He never changes. He is permanent in who He is.

E.   The most important name of God in the Old Testament reveals the truth of His eternity. YHWH refers to the I AM WHO I AM, indicating that God is the Self-Existent One.

And God said to Moses, "I AM WHO I AM." And He said, "Thus you shall say to the children of Israel, 'I AM has sent me to you.'" (Exodus 3:14)

IV.   THE ETERNITY OF GOD—A DIVINE ATTRIBUTE

A.   *God is his own eternity. He is not eternal by grant, and the disposal of any other, but by nature and essence. The eternity of God is nothing else but the duration of God; and the duration of God is nothing else but his existence enduring. If eternity were anything distinct from God, and not of the essence of God, then there would be something which was not God, necessary to perfect God. As immortality is the great perfection of a rational creature, so eternity is the choice perfection of God...* [3]

B.   God made all things for Himself that He might disclose all that He is to His people. This disclosure is called the knowledge of God. God does not posses the description of the attribute; He is that which the attribute describes. For example, God does not have love; God is love. Similarly, God's eternity is another of His attributes.

C.   What God discloses or reveals about Himself is an attribute. The attributes of God are not limited to the ones that are referenced in the Word of God. The infinitude of God insists that He has an infinite amount of attributes that will not be disclosed until the age to come when we see God face to face.

D.   *An attribute, as we can know it, is a mental concept, an intellectual response to God's self-revelation. It is an answer to a question, the reply God makes to our interrogation concerning Himself.* [4]

---

3   Ibid., p. 285.
4   Tozer, A.W. *The Knowledge of the Holy* (San Francisco: HarperSanFrancisco, 1961), p. 13.

*And the L*ORD *passed before him and proclaimed, "The L*ORD*, the L*ORD *God, merciful and gracious, longsuffering, and abounding in goodness and truth, keeping mercy for thousands, forgiving iniquity and transgression and sin, by no means clearing the guilty, visiting the iniquity of the fathers upon the children and the children's children to the third and the fourth generation." (Exodus 34:6–7)*

E.   A divine attribute is not a part of who God is; it is the whole of Him. He cannot be fragmented into parts. For example, God is not a sum total of all of His attributes, but rather He **is**.

*Then Moses said to God, "Indeed, when I come to the children of Israel and say to them, 'The God of your fathers has sent me to you,' and they say to me, 'What is His **name**?' what shall I say to them?" And God said to Moses, "I AM WHO I AM." And He said, "Thus you shall say to the children of Israel, 'I AM has sent me to you.'" (Exodus 3:13–15, emphasis added)*

F.   *A man is the sum of his parts and his character the sum of the traits that compose it. These traits vary from man to man and may from time to time vary from themselves within the same man. Human character is not constant because the traits or qualities that constitute it are unstable . . . God exists in Himself and of Himself. His being He owes to no one. His substance is **indivisible**. He has parts but is **single** in His **unitary** being.*[5]

G.   *The doctrine of the divine unity means not only that there is but one God; it means also that God is **simple**, **uncomplex**, one with Himself. The **harmony** of His being is the result not of a perfect **balance** of parts but of the **absence** of parts. Between His attributes no contradiction can exist. He need not suspend one to exercise another, for in Him all His attributes are one. All of God does all that God does; He does not divide Himself to perform a work, but works in the total unity of His being.*[6]

H.   Eternity is the realm of God. It is not a place, setting, or context that can be measured. Rather, it is the very essence and nature of God. When we are speaking of eternity, we are talking about God Himself. Eternity is an attribute of God.

---

5   Ibid., p. 14–15. Emphasis added.
6   Tozer, A.W. *The Knowledge of the Holy* (San Francisco: HarperSanFrancisco, 1961), p. 14–15. Emphasis added.

I.   God's eternity stretches from before the beginning of Genesis 1 and endures forever. God is not temporal; He is eternal. From eternity to eternity He is God.

*For thus says **the High and Lofty One who inhabits eternity**, whose name is **Holy: "I dwell in the high and holy place,** with him who has a contrite and humble spirit, to revive the spirit of the humble, and to revive the heart of the contrite ones." (Isaiah 57:15, emphasis added)*

V.   THE DOCTRINE OF ETERNITY IS COMFORT IN TRIBULATION (ISAIAH 40)

*"**Comfort**, yes, **comfort** My people!" (Isaiah 40:1, emphasis added)*

***Let not your heart be troubled**; you believe in God, believe also in Me. **In My Father's house are many mansions**; if it were not so, I would have told you. I go to prepare a place for you. (John 14:1–2, emphasis added)*

A.   The eternity of God speaks of His constancy.

B.   *The eternity of God is the foundation of the stability of the covenant, the great comfort of a Christian . . . Eternity is a negative attribute, and is a denying of God any measures of time, as immensity is a denying of him any bounds of place.*[7]

C.   The Lord is raising up voices at the end of the age that, having encountered the reality of God's eternity, will proclaim this revelation. Isaiah 40 is a prophecy concerning these voices of eternity.

D.   Isaiah 40:1–2: Call to comfort the people of God.

E.   Isaiah 40:3–5: The promise to raise up prophetic voices that will proclaim eternity.

F.   Isaiah 40:6–9: The good news of eternity.

G.   Isaiah 40:10–28: The transcendence and eternity of God.

   1.   40:10: The coming of God.

---

7   Charnock, Stephen. *The Existence and Attributes of God, Volume One* (Grand Rapids: Baker Books, 2005), p. 279, 281.

2.   40:11: The tenderness of the eternal God.

3.   40:12: The greatness of Creator God.

4.   40:13–14: The eternal wisdom of divine administration.

5.   40:15–17: The eternally blessed and only Sovereign over the nations.

6.   40:18–20: The eternally uncreated God.

7.   40:21–26: The Almighty God.

8.   40:27–28: The discouraged invited to consider the eternity of God (John 14:1).

9.   40:28: The everlasting God.

H.   Isaiah 40:29–31: Call to partake of the knowledge of God.

VI.   THE ETERNITY OF GOD

A.   He is the Alpha—the Godhead is without beginning. He (the Holy Trinity) has always been. He existed before all of creation.

In the beginning God created the heavens and the earth. The earth was without form, and void; and darkness was on the face of the deep. And the Spirit of God was hovering over the face of the waters. Then God said, "Let there be light"; and there was light. (Genesis 1:1–3)

*The L*ORD *possessed me at **the beginning** of His way, **before His works of old**. I have been **established from everlasting, from the beginning, before** there was ever an earth. When there were no depths I was brought forth, when there were no fountains abounding with water. **Before** the mountains were settled, before the hills, I was brought forth; **while as yet He had not made the earth or the fields, or the primal dust of the world**. When He prepared the heavens, I was there, when He drew a circle on the face of the deep, when He established the clouds above, when He strengthened the fountains of the deep, when He assigned to the sea its limit, so that the waters would not transgress His command, when He marked out the foundations of the earth, then I was beside Him as a master craftsman; and I was daily His delight, rejoicing always before Him, rejoicing in His inhabited world, and my delight was with the sons of men. (Proverbs 8:22–31, emphasis added)*

B. The Godhead is the Omega—God in Himself is the beginning and the end of all things, but He Himself is without end.

C. God is the I AM WHO I AM. YHWH is the never-ending, never-changing, self-sustaining, uncreated, eternal God of all creation. God is the same yesterday, today and forever. He is the eternal present tense knowing, not past or future, but the eternal present tense.

*Jesus Christ **is the same** yesterday, today, and forever. (Hebrews 13:8, emphasis added)*

*Every good gift and every perfect gift is from above, and comes down from the Father of lights, **with whom there is no variation or shadow of turning.** (James 1:17, emphasis added)*

*I will declare the decree: The L*ORD *has said to Me, "You are My Son, **today I have begotten** You." (Psalm 2:7, emphasis added)*

D. God stands alone. There is none before Him or after Him; He has no successor.

*I urge you in the sight of God who gives life to all things, and before Christ Jesus who witnessed the good confession before Pontius Pilate, that you keep this commandment without spot, blameless until our Lord Jesus Christ's appearing, which He will manifest in His own time, He who is the blessed and **only Potentate, the King of kings and Lord of lords, who alone has immortality**, dwelling in unapproachable light, whom no man has seen or can see, to whom be honor and **everlasting power**. Amen. (1 Timothy 6:13–16, emphasis added)*

E.   There is nothing that can be added to God or taken away from Him.

*For in Him dwells all the fullness of the Godhead bodily; and **you are complete in Him**, who is the head of all principality and power. (Colossians 2:9–10, emphasis added)*

F.   God is great beyond measure.

*Oh, the depth of the riches both of the wisdom and knowledge of God! **How unsearchable are His judgments and His ways past finding out!** (Romans 11:33, emphasis added)*

Session Eleven: The Terrifying Beauty of God

I. ONE THING I DESIRE OF THE LORD: LONGING FOR FASCINATION AND BEAUTY

A. *It is no wonder that deep, divinely infused contemplative immersion in the indwelling Trinity issues in an unspeakable delight that can trigger ecstasy. Our saints, Bernard or Catherine, Teresa or John of the Cross (as well as those who follow their teaching), are not exaggerating when they declare that they cannot describe "the least part" (John's expression) of what they experience. There is nothing comparable on the earth.*

One step further, a long step beyond even the inexpressible heights of mystical prayer on earth: the beatific vision in glory. This direct seeing of the endlessly lovely Trinity face to face, and without any mediating concept or idea whatever, is eternally, absolutely unending. We shall never exhaust the wonder, the dazzlingly enthralling drinking of limitless Beauty. Indeed, "eye has not seen, nor ear heard, nor can we even imagine what God has prepared for those who love him" (1 Cor 2:9). The reason is that he has prepared himself, endless enthrallment. Heaven is eternal ecstasy.[1]

B. God has put eternity in our hearts (Ecclesiastes 3:11). This reality expresses itself in various divinely designed and orchestrated longings in our hearts. There are several longings of the human heart that flow out of the truth that eternity has been put into our hearts. Our beings were designed with a craving that can only be satisfied by the Holy.[2]

C. King David and his son, King Solomon, both give us the theology of the eternal craving of the human heart, which will only be satisfied by the eternal. We all have a desire to be fascinated and have a longing for beauty. This cry for fascination and longing for beauty is answered by the revelation of the Beautiful and the divine drama that is around the throne of God.

*One thing I have desired of the LORD, that will I seek: that I may dwell in the house of the LORD all the days of my life, **to behold the beauty of the LORD**, and **to inquire in His temple**. (Psalm 27:4, emphasis added)*

---

1   Dubay, Thomas. *The Evidential Power of Beauty* (San Francisco: Ignatius Press, 1999), p. 43–44.
2   Bickle, Mike and Deborah Hiebert. *The Seven Longings of the Human Heart* (Kansas City: Forerunner Books, 2006).

> *He has made everything beautiful in its time. Also **He has put eternity in their hearts**, except that no one can find out the work that God does from beginning to end. (Ecclesiastes 3:11, emphasis added)*

D.   *In his masterpiece,* The Brothers Karamazov, *Fyodor Dostoyevski placed on the lips of one of his characters the observation that "beauty is the battlefield where God and Satan contend with each other for the hearts of men." The one is supreme Glory (the biblical name for supereminent beauty); the other is supreme ugliness. Though our free wills make the choice, it is beauty that provides the powerful attraction to the only victory that ultimately matters in this peak of all combats.*[3]

E.   Hans Urs von Balthasar once said, "Every experience of beauty points to infinity." When we encounter beauty, it produces wonder, awe and delight and awakens a deeper longing for mystery in our hearts. Beauty grasps, stuns, bewilders and arrests the heart.

F.   In his book *The Evidential Power of Beauty*, Thomas Dubay highlights three necessary ingredients for beauty to be what it is:[4]

1.   Simplicity—referred to by Dubay as "a freedom from superfluities, useless accretions, and needless complications." There is nothing lacking, nothing superfluous.

2.   Harmony—unity and wholeness.

3.   Brilliance—a glowing quality.

II.   HOLY, HOLY, HOLY IS THE LORD

> ***Above it stood seraphim**; each one had six wings: with two he covered his face, with two he covered his feet, and with two he flew. **And one cried to another and said: "Holy, holy, holy is the Lord of hosts**; the whole earth is full of His glory!" (Isaiah 6:2–3, emphasis added)*

> ***The four living creatures**, each having six wings, were full of eyes around and within. And they do not rest day or night, saying: **"Holy, holy, holy, Lord God Almighty**, who was and is and is to come!" (Revelation 4:8, emphasis added)*

---

3   Dubay, Thomas. *The Evidential Power of Beauty*. (San Francisco: Ignatius Press, 1999), p. 20.
4   Ibid., p. 39–40.

A.   The very foundation and essence of the Being of God is His transcendence. He is Holy. The holiness of God speaks of His of otherness. God is wholly other than any thing that is created or common.

B.   As John N. Oswalt states, "Thus, holiness is distinctness, the distinctness of the divine from all other things. There is no reason to believe that the term had any moral connotation about it at the outset."[5]

C.   The holiness of the Lord is in reference to the transcendent beauty of who He is. God is the most beautiful and magnificent Being we will ever know.

D.   The premier song that is being sung around the throne of God is the song of the transcendent beauty of the Lord: "Holy, holy, holy is the Lord God Almighty!" (Revelation 4:8). The transcendence of the Lord speaks of the fact that the qualities He possesses in His being and in His nature are infinitely superior to all that He has created whether in Heaven or on the earth. In His being, God is infinitely higher then everything created or common. This height is in reference not to a geographical distance, but it speaks of the quality of His existence, His worth that is infinite in its scope.

E.   *Yet we must not compare the being of God with any other as we just now compared the mountain with the child. We must not think of God as highest in an ascending order of beings, starting with the single cell and going on up from the fish to the bird to the animal to man to angel to cherub to God. This would be to grant God eminence, even preeminence, but that is not enough; we must grant Him transcendence in the fullest meaning of that meaning.*[6]

F.   Transcendence is the very "foundation" and essence of His being.

---

5   Oswalt, John N. *The Book of Isaiah: Chapters 1–39* (Grand Rapids, MI: William B. Eerdmans Publishing Company: 1986), p. 180.

6   Tozer, A.W. *The Knowledge of the Holy* (San Francisco: HarperSanFransisco, 1961), p. 70.

Where do you find any other attribute trebled in the praises of it, as this (Isa vi. 3)? "Holy, holy, holy is the Lord of hosts, the whole earth is full of his glory;" and (Rev. vi. 8), "The four beast rest not day and night, saying, Holy, holy, holy, Lord God Almighty," &c. His power or sovereignty, as Lord of hosts, is but once mentioned, but with an eternal repetition of his holiness. Do you hear, in any angelical song, any other perfection of the Divine Nature thrice repeated [Trisagion]? Where do we read of the crying out Eternal, eternal, eternal; or, Faithful, faithful, faithful, Lord God of Hosts? Whatsoever other attribute is left out, this God would have to fill the mouths of angels and blessed spirits for ever in heaven.[7]

III.   HE ALONE IS HOLY BUT IMPARTS HIS BEAUTY

No one is holy like the LORD, for there is none besides You, nor is there any rock like our God. (1 Samuel 2:2)

A.   God alone is holy, but He imparts the beauty that He possesses; therefore, there are holy angels, the people of God are holy and we are a holy nation (1 Peter 2:9).

B.   *. . . As there is none good but God, so none holy but God. No creature can be essentially holy, because mutable; holiness is the substance of God, but a quality and accident in a creature. God is infinitely holy, creatures finitely holy. He is holy from himself, creatures are holy by derivation from him. He is not only holy, but holiness; holiness in the highest degree, is his sole prerogative. As the highest heaven is called the heaven of heavens, because it embraceth in its circle all the heavens, and contains the magnitude of them, and hath a greater vastness above all that it encloseth, so is God the Holy of holies; he contains the holiness of all creatures put together, and infinitely more.*[8]

*Around the Throne were **twenty-four thrones**, and on the thrones I saw twenty-four elders sitting, clothed in white **robes**; and they had **crowns** of gold on their heads. (Revelation 4:4, emphasis added)*

C.   There are significant emotional implications to knowing that our destiny in God is to be enthroned, robed and crowned. This causes us to feel great security, dignity and beauty, and we view God and ourselves differently and worship with all of our hearts.

---

7   Charnock, Stephen. *The Existence and Attributes of God, Volume Two* (Grand Rapids: Baker Books, 2005), p. 112.

8   Charnock, Stephen. *The Existence and Attributes of God, Volume Two* (Grand Rapids: Baker Books, 2005), p. 116.

D.   The beauty God possesses is the very beauty that He imparts to His elders and all His people.

> *. . . **To give them beauty** for ashes . . . (Isaiah 61:3, emphasis added)*

E.   God's beauty is seen in His great kindness to exalt His former enemies to such heights so as to reign as His Bride. We stand in amazement at how important our lives are to God.

> *. . .When we were **enemies** we were reconciled to God through . . . His Son . . . (Romans 5:10, emphasis added)*

> *. . . How shall we escape (judgment) if we neglect **so great a salvation** . . . "You have **crowned him** (the redeemed) **with glory and honor, and set him over** the works of Your hands" . . . For it was **fitting** (made sense, was reasonable) for Him (the Father) . . . in **bringing many sons to glory**, to make the captain of their salvation (Jesus) perfect through sufferings. (Hebrews 2:3, 7–10, emphasis and parenthetical comments added)*

F.   God has raised up an excellent Bride who is the glory of Jesus, her heavenly Bridegroom.

> *An excellent wife is the **crown** of her husband . . . (Proverbs 12:4, emphasis added)*

G.   The greatness and glory of God's salvation for weak and broken people is indescribable.

> *Eye has not seen, nor ear heard, **nor have entered into the heart of man** the things which God has prepared for those who love Him. (1 Corinthians 2:9, emphasis added)*

IV.   THE BEAUTY OF THE LORD AND THE ORACLES OF FELLOWSHIP

A.   Jesus prayed that the Kingdom of God would be on Earth as it is in Heaven. One of the realities seen in Heaven is the conversation of the angels around the throne, which revolves around the subject of God's holiness.

> *Above it stood **seraphim**; each one had six wings: with two he covered his face, with two he covered his feet, and with two he flew. And **one cried to another and said**: "Holy, holy, holy is the LORD of hosts; The whole earth is full of His glory!" (Isaiah 6:2–3, emphasis added)*

*The **four living creatures**, each having six wings, were full of eyes around and within. **And they do not rest day or night, saying**: "Holy, holy, holy, Lord God Almighty, Who was and is and is to come!" (Revelation 4:8, emphasis added)*

*To them it was revealed that, not to themselves, but to us they were ministering the things which now have been reported to you through those who have **preached the gospel to you by the Holy Spirit sent from heaven—things which angels desire to look into.** (1 Peter 1:12, emphasis added)*

B.   I believe the Lord's vision is to see this same dynamic released on the earth now in part within the church and then in full in the age to come. The Scripture often calls for holy speech and grace-filled words. When the revelation of the transcendence of God touches our inner man, it transforms our communication in prayer, worship, fellowship and preaching.

C.   The speaking of holy things will fill our inner man with worship and adoration unto the Lord. This is seen in the writings of Paul, as he would dictate letters to his scribe. Paul would often explode in praise and adoration to the Lord (known as a doxology).

Oh, the depth of the riches both of the wisdom and knowledge of God! How unsearchable are His judgments and His ways past finding out! "For who has known the mind of the LORD? Or who has become His counselor?" "Or who has first given to Him and it shall be repaid to him?" For of Him and through Him and to Him are all things, to whom be glory forever. Amen. (Romans 11:33–36)

. . . Which He will manifest in His own time, He who is the blessed and only Potentate, the King of kings and Lord of lords, who alone has immortality, dwelling in unapproachable light, whom no man has seen or can see, to whom be honor and everlasting power. Amen. (1 Timothy 6:15–16)

Now to Him who is able to keep you from stumbling, and to present you faultless before the presence of His glory with exceeding joy, to God our Savior, who alone is wise, be glory and majesty, dominion and power, both now and forever. Amen. (Jude:24–25)

To Him who loved us and washed us from our sins in His own blood, and has made us kings and priests to His God and Father, to Him be glory and dominion forever and ever. Amen.

Behold, He is coming with clouds, and every eye will see Him, even they who pierced Him. And all the tribes of the earth will mourn because of Him. Even so, Amen. (Revelation 1:5–7)

D.   Wholesome speech impacts our fellowship with other believers.

If anyone speaks, let him speak as the oracles of God. If anyone ministers, let him do it as with the ability which God supplies, that in all things God may be glorified through Jesus Christ, to whom belong the glory and the dominion forever and ever. Amen. (1 Peter 4:11, emphasis added)

If anyone teaches otherwise and does not consent to wholesome words, even the words of our Lord Jesus Christ, and to the doctrine which accords with godliness, he is proud, knowing nothing, but is obsessed with disputes and arguments over words, from which come envy, strife, reviling, evil suspicions, useless wranglings of men of corrupt minds and destitute of the truth, who suppose that godliness is a means of gain. From such withdraw yourself. (1 Timothy 6:3–5, emphasis added)

E.   Preaching Christ to unbelievers is most effective when the preacher has revelation of the beauty of the Lord.

For we do not preach ourselves, but Christ Jesus the Lord, and ourselves your bondservants for Jesus' sake. For it is the God who commanded light to shine out of darkness, who has shone in our hearts to give the light of the knowledge of the glory of God in the face of Jesus Christ. (2 Corinthians 4:5–6, emphasis added)

Him we preach, warning every man and teaching every man in all wisdom, that we may present every man perfect in Christ Jesus. To this end I also labor, striving according to His working which works in me mightily. (Colossians 1:28–29, emphasis added)

F.   Revelation of mystery is necessary for divine enablement to speak of eternal glories.

But the LORD said to me: "Do not say, 'I am a youth,' for you shall go to all to whom I send you, and whatever I command you, you shall speak. Do not be afraid of their faces, for I am with you to deliver you," says the LORD. Then the LORD put forth His hand and touched my mouth, and the LORD said to me: "Behold, I have put My words in your mouth." (Jeremiah 1:7–9, emphasis added)

*To me, who am less than the least of all the saints, **this grace was given, that I should preach** among the Gentiles **the unsearchable riches of Christ** . . . (Ephesians 3:8, emphasis added)*

V. THE BEAUTY AND THE DREAD OF THE LORD

A. The transcendence of the Lord reveals the otherness of God. The nature and quality of His being is infinitely other than anything that is created or common. The dread and fear of the Lord comes when creation encounters His majestic splendor. I like to call the transcendence of God His terrifying beauty.

B. We were meant to be gripped, fascinated enthralled and to tremble before infinite beauty. It is the primary thing for which we were created.

The LORD of hosts, Him you shall hallow; let Him be your fear, and let Him be your dread. (Isaiah 8:13)

Wisdom and knowledge will be the stability of your times, and the strength of salvation; the fear of the LORD is His treasure. (Isaiah 33:6)

VI. THE THRONE-CHARIOT OF GOD

A. The government and sovereignty of God was revealed to Ezekiel in the hour of Israel's crisis and great confusion (Ezekiel 1). Similarly, the revelation of the beauty of God will serve as the source of strength and hope for the Church of Jesus Christ and the nation of Israel at the end of the age.

B. One of the greatest questions that rises up in the human heart in an hour of crisis is "Where is God?" The reality of the storm of God reveals to us that God is active and not static. Storms are a great source of energy, power, intensity and fascination. The human response to a storm usually is that of fear and fascination.

C. God's grace was seen in His contention with and pursuit of Israel while they were still in exile. Part of the manifestation of the jealousy of God is relentless pursuit. **The thunder of the storm** is seen in the reality of the Cross, where God pursued us by becoming a human even unto death. There is a Man above the throne in the whirlwind, indicating that the fullness of the jealousy of God would be revealed in His incarnation and in the Cross of Christ.

D.   The whirlwind of God reminded Israel of the jealousy of the Bridegroom Judge. God reminded Israel of the covenant He made with them in the wilderness. I believe that the whirlwind speaks of the garments of YWHW's betrothal and is a picture of how He will return to Israel when He marries the land again.

*Moreover the word of the LORD came to me, saying, "Go and cry in the hearing of Jerusalem, saying, 'Thus says the LORD: "I remember you, the kindness of your youth, **the love of your betrothal, when you went after Me in the wilderness,** in a land not sown."' (Jeremiah 2:1–2, emphasis added)*

*"Now therefore, if you will indeed obey My voice and **keep My covenant, then you shall be a special treasure to Me above all people; for all the earth is Mine.** And **you** shall be to Me a kingdom of priests and a holy nation." These are the words which you shall speak to the children of Israel. (Exodus 19:5–6, emphasis added)*

*Then it came to pass on the third day, in the morning, that there were **thunderings and lightnings, and a thick cloud on the mountain** (storm theophany, whirlwind); and the sound of the trumpet was very loud, so that all the people who were in the camp trembled. (Exodus 19:16, emphasis added, parenthetical comment added)*

But I will kindle a fire in the wall of Rabbah, and it shall devour its palaces, amid shouting in the day of battle, and a tempest in the day of the whirlwind (the day of the Lord, Second Coming). (Amos 1:14, parenthetical comment added)

*You shall no longer be termed Forsaken, **nor shall your land any more be termed Desolate;** but you shall be called Hephzibah, and your land Beulah; for the LORD delights in you, **and your land shall be married** (at the Second Coming). (Isaiah 62:4, emphasis added, parenthetical comments added)*

E.   The whirlwind, or storm, that Ezekiel encountered is also known as the Throne-Chariot of God. I believe that the whirlwind of God and His chariot are associated.

*Then it happened, as they continued on and talked, that suddenly **a chariot of fire appeared with horses of fire,** and separated the two of them; and **Elijah went up by a whirlwind into heaven.** And Elisha saw it, and he cried out, "My father, my father, **the chariot of Israel and its horsemen!"** So he saw him no more. And he took hold of his own clothes and tore them into two pieces. (2 Kings 2:11–12, emphasis added)*

*For behold, **the Lord will come with fire and with His chariots, like a whirlwind,** to render His anger with fury, and His rebuke with flames of fire. (Isaiah 66:15, emphasis added)*

F.   The whirlwind of God is a means of transport into the realm of glory where the counsels are revealed, the deep things of God, the thoughts and intents of His heart. The whirlwind is the realm where we get filled with the knowledge of His will. All end-time prophetic messengers must experience this reality, and do so by eating the scroll (Colossians 1:9; Ezekiel 2:9–3:4).

*And it came to pass, when the Lord was about to **take up Elijah** (mode of transportation in the spirit realm) **into heaven by a whirlwind,** that Elijah went with Elisha from Gilgal. (2 Kings 2:1, emphasis added, parenthetical comment added)*

*I saw still another mighty angel coming down from heaven, clothed with a **cloud.** And a **rainbow** was on his head, his **face was like the sun,** and his **feet like pillars of fire.** (Revelation 10:1, emphasis added)*

G.   God speaks from the whirlwind (storm). This is precedented throughout the Old Testament.

*And the Lord said to Moses, "Behold, I come to you in **the thick cloud,** that the people may hear **when I speak with you,** and believe you forever." (Exodus 19:9, emphasis added)*

*You called in trouble, and I delivered you; **I answered you in the secret place of thunder;** I tested you at the waters of Meribah. (Psalm 81:7, emphasis added)*

*Then the Lord **answered** Job out of the **whirlwind,** and said . . . (Job 38:1, emphasis added)*

*Then the Lord **answered** Job out of the **whirlwind,** and said . . . (Job 40:6, emphasis added)*

*The **voice of Your thunder** was in the **whirlwind;** the lightnings lit up the world; the earth trembled and shook. (Psalm 77:18, emphasis added)*

. . . And cried with a loud voice, as when a lion roars. When he (the angel from the storm) *cried out,* **seven thunders uttered their voices.** *Now when the seven thunders uttered their voices, I was about to write; but I heard a voice from heaven saying to me,* **"Seal up the things which the seven thunders uttered, and do not write them."** *(Revelation 10:3–4, emphasis and parenthetical comment added)*

H. God manifests His jealousy in judgment and establishes His eternal purpose by the whirlwind. In the whirlwind, we encounter the zeal of God to see His will accomplished on the earth. I view it as a torrent of desire because in it we encounter the desires of God.

When the **whirlwind** *passes by,* **the wicked is no more,** *but the righteous has an everlasting foundation. (Proverbs 10:25, emphasis added)*

For behold, **the Lord will come with fire and with His chariots, like a whirlwind, to render His anger with fury, and His rebuke with flames of fire.** *For* **by** *fire and by His sword the Lord will judge all flesh; and the slain of the Lord shall be many. (Isaiah 66:15–16, emphasis added)*

Behold, a **whirlwind** *of the Lord has gone forth in fury—* **a violent whirlwind!** *It will fall violently on the head of the wicked.* **The anger of the Lord** *will not turn back* **until He has executed and performed the thoughts of His heart.** *In the latter days you will understand it perfectly. (Jeremiah 23:19–20, emphasis added)*

. . . Having made known to us **the mystery of His will, according to His good pleasure** *which He* **purposed in Himself,** *that in the dispensation of the fullness of the times He might gather together in one all things in Christ, both which are in heaven and which are on earth—in Him. (Ephesians 1:9–10, emphasis added)*

Father, I desire *that they also whom You gave Me* **may be with Me where I am, that they may behold My glory** *which You have given Me; for You loved Me before the foundation of the world. (John 17:24, emphasis added)*

Session Twelve: The Transcendent Beauty of God (Ezekiel 1)

I. THE COMPONENTS OF THE SECOND COMING IN THE THRONE-CHARIOT OF GOD

A. The Day of the Lord, according to Amos 1:14, is also called the day of the whirlwind. The term not only describes the turmoil that the Day of the Lord will bring to the earth, but also the manner and the mode of Jesus' second coming.

B. In the Old Testament, Jesus came and went in the context of smoke and clouds, depicting His glory (the fire storm of Ezekiel 1). New Testament references to His second coming also describe Him coming on glory-clouds with glory-smoke. He will come traveling on His Throne-Chariot in the divine whirlwind.

C. A great cloud—the weight of glory

*But I will kindle a fire in the wall of Rabbah, and it shall devour its palaces, amid shouting in **the day of battle,** and a tempest in **the day of the whirlwind.** (Amos 1:14, emphasis added)*

*Then I looked, and behold, a whirlwind was coming out of the north, **a great cloud with raging fire engulfing itself;** and brightness was all around it and radiating out of its midst like the color of amber, out of the midst of the fire. (Ezekiel 1:4, emphasis added)*

*Then the sign of the Son of Man will appear in heaven, and then all the tribes of the earth will mourn, and they will see the **Son of Man coming on the clouds of heaven** with power and great glory. (Matthew 24:30, emphasis added)*

*Jesus said to him, "It is as you said. Nevertheless, I say to you, hereafter you will see the Son of Man sitting at the right hand of the Power, and **coming on the clouds of heaven.**" (Matthew 26:64, emphasis added)*

*. . . The stars of heaven will fall, and the powers in the heavens will be shaken. Then they will see the **Son of Man coming in the clouds** with great power and glory. (Mark 13:25–26, emphasis added)*

*Jesus said, "I am. And you will see the Son of Man sitting at the right hand of the Power, and **coming with the clouds of heaven.**" (Mark 14:62, emphasis added)*

*Then they will see the Son of Man **coming in a cloud with power and great glory.** (Luke 21:27, emphasis added)*

*Then we who are alive and remain shall be **caught up together with them in the clouds to meet the Lord in the air.** And thus we shall always be with the Lord. (1 Thessalonians 4:17, emphasis added)*

*Behold, **He is coming with clouds,** and every eye will see Him, even they who pierced Him. And all the tribes of the earth will mourn because of Him. Even so, Amen. (Revelation 1:7, emphasis added)*

And they heard a loud voice from heaven saying to them, "Come up here." And they ascended to heaven in a cloud, and their enemies saw them. (Revelation 11:12, emphasis added)

*Then I looked, and behold, **a white cloud,** and **on the cloud sat One like the Son of Man,** having on His head a golden crown, and in His hand a sharp sickle. And another angel came out of the temple, crying with a loud voice **to Him who sat on the cloud,** "Thrust in Your sickle and reap, for the time has come for You to reap, for the harvest of the earth is ripe." So He who sat on the cloud thrust in His sickle on the earth, and the earth was reaped. (Revelation 14:14–16, emphasis added)*

D.   With raging fire—the realm of the jealousy of God

*. . . When the Lord Jesus is revealed from heaven with His mighty angels, **in flaming fire taking vengeance** on those who do not know God, and on those who do not obey the gospel of our Lord Jesus Christ. (2 Thessalonians 1:7–8, emphasis added)*

E.   Brightness was all around it and radiating out of its midst like the color of amber.

*And then the lawless one will be revealed, whom the Lord will consume with the breath of His mouth and destroy **with the brightness of His coming.** (2 Thessalonians 2:8, emphasis added)*

*. . . **Who being the brightness of His glory** and the express image of His person, and upholding all things by the word of His power, when He had by Himself purged our sins, sat down at the right hand of the Majesty on high . . . (Hebrews 1:3, emphasis added)*

*Then the sign of the Son of Man will appear in heaven, and then all the tribes of the earth will mourn, and they will see the Son of Man coming on the clouds of heaven **with power and great glory.** (Matthew 24:30, emphasis added)*

*Then they will see the Son of Man coming in the clouds **with great power and glory.** (Mark 13:26, emphasis added)*

*Then they will see the Son of Man coming in a cloud **with power and great glory.** (Luke 21:27, emphasis added)*

*These shall be punished with everlasting destruction from the presence of the Lord and **from the glory of His power.** (2 Thessalonians 1:9, emphasis added)*

F.   The likeness of four **living** creatures—the realm of the angels

*For the Son of Man will come in the glory of His Father **with His angels,** and then He will reward each according to his works. (Matthew 16:27, emphasis added)*

***And He will send His angels** with a great sound of a trumpet, and they will gather together His elect from the four winds, from one end of heaven to the other. (Matthew 24:31, emphasis added)*

*When the Son of Man comes in His glory, **and all the holy angels with Him,** then He will sit on the throne of His glory. (Matthew 25:31, emphasis added)*

G.   A flash of lightning—God's divine action and splendor

*For as **the lightning comes from the east and flashes to the west,** so also will the coming of the Son of Man be. (Matthew 24:27, emphasis added)*

For as the lightning that flashes out of one part under heaven shines to the other part under heaven, so also the Son of Man will be in His day. (Luke 17:24)

II. THE SEVEN REALMS OF GLORY

A. The basic structure of the Throne-Chariot of God consists of two general realities: connecting Earth and Heaven, which are separated by the sapphire pavement (Exodus 24:9–10). The storm also has three basic realms: exterior, interior and superior. The Throne-Chariot reveals seven basic realms, or layers, of the glory of God. I believe that these seven realms of God appeared to the nation of Israel in Exodus 19, 20, 24:1–10.

B. Ezekiel 1:4–21—the earthly reality

C. Ezekiel 1:22–28—the heavenly reality

D. Ezekiel 1:4—exterior dimension

E. Ezekiel 1:5–21—interior dimension

F. Ezekiel 1:22–28—interior above or superior dimension

G. **The earthly reality,** or that which interacts with the realm of the natural, consists of the cloud (1:4), the four living creatures (1:5–14) and the wheels (1:15–21). **The heavenly reality,** or that which interacts with the realm of the heavens, consists of the sapphire expanse (1:22–25), the sapphire throne (1:26), the glory of the Son of Man (1:27) and God's enduring mercy (1:28).

III. A GREAT CLOUD (1:4)

*Then I looked, and behold, a **whirlwind was coming out of the north, a great cloud with raging fire engulfing** itself; and **brightness was all around it and radiating out of its midst like the color of amber,** out of the midst of the fire. (Ezekiel 1:4, emphasis added)*

*. . . So that the priests could not continue ministering because of the cloud; for the glory of the Lord filled the house of God. Then Solomon spoke: "**The Lord said He would dwell in the dark cloud."** (2 Chronicles 5:14–6:1, emphasis added)*

A. There are four components of the great cloud.

1. It is a great cloud with **raging fire.**

2. The raging fire **engulfs itself** (fire flashes back and forth). Ezekiel saw fire like molten metal exuding out of the dark cloud of glory, contained by it and engulfing it all at the same time. This fire is flashing back and forth like an ocean tide. The fire that goes in and out of the cloud is like molten metal or liquid fire. It is the realm of everlasting burnings, and Ezekiel is invited to stand and see the beauty of YHWH. Undoubtedly this whole realm is set on fire. Ezekiel encountered the realm of the jealousy of God (Deuteronomy 4:24; Song of Songs 5:10; Revelation 4:3).

3. There is **brightness all around** the raging fire like the color amber (Psalm 27:4, 104:2; John 1:1–3; 2 Corinthians 4:6; 1 Timothy 6:16; Hebrews 1:3; Revelation 1:16, 4:3).

4. The brightness like the color amber was also **coming out** of the fire like molten metal. This divine cloud is swallowed up and saturated by the liquid fire of God. This fire is possibly the fire the flows from the throne of God in Daniel 7. The fire swallows up the cloud, but the cloud swallows up and saturates the fire. The fire comes from out of the midst of the cloud, going back and forth, engulfing the very cloud from which it came. The fire violently lashes out of the cloud then pulls back into the cloud.

IV. THE LIVING CREATURES (1:5–14)

A. These living creatures are those called cherubim in Ezekiel 10. I believe that they are guardians of the glory of God. In my opinion, these are not the same as the living creatures, or the seraphim, of Isaiah 6 and Revelation 4–5 because the cherubim are underneath the throne and the sapphire expanse rather than above them.

B. The first time cherubim are mentioned in the Word of God, they are seen as guardians of the Garden of Eden, prohibiting entrance and access to the Tree of Life.

So He drove out the man; and He placed cherubim at the east of the garden of Eden, and a flaming sword which turned every way, to guard the way to the tree of life. (Genesis 3:24)

C. Before his fall, Satan was an anointed covering, or guarding, cherub. The very thing of which he was guardian, he wanted for himself.

*You were the **anointed cherub who covers;** I established you; you were on the holy mountain of God; **you walked back and forth in the midst of fiery stones.** (Ezekiel 28:14, emphasis added)*

*By the abundance of your trading You became filled with violence within, and you sinned; therefore I cast you as a profane thing out of the mountain of God; and I destroyed you, **O covering cherub,** from the midst of the fiery stones. (Ezekiel 28:16, emphasis added)*

D. We see later that these angelic beings are dynamically related to the movement and the direction of the wheels under the guidance of the Spirit as though they carry this divine vehicle, which conveys the glory and the throne of Christ. It is with zeal that they guard and participate in the movements of the sovereign government of God.

E. The description of the living creatures reflects aspects of the glory of God.

   1. The frame of the four living creatures has the appearance of a human, indicating that humanity is God's crowning glory of creation.

   2. The four living creatures each have four faces.

      a. The face of a lion—the majesty of God

      b. The face of an ox—the strength of God

      c. The face of an eagle—the swiftness and splendor of God

      d. The face of a man—God's desire for humanity

   3. Their legs are straight with gleaming hooves, indicating that they are steadfast in the presence of God and they stand on holy ground.

      *And the angel answered and said to him, "I am **Gabriel, who stands in the presence of God,** and was sent to speak to you and bring you these glad tidings." (Luke 1:19, emphasis added)*

   4. The four living creatures have hands under their wings, and the wings of one being touch those of another.

5.   The movement of these beings is forward, which speaks of the stalwart focus and readiness of these beings to obey the voice of the Almighty.

6.   These beings have four wings. With two wings they cover their frame in reference to the glory of God, and with the other two they could possibly be carrying the platform on which the throne is seated. I think that in some ways, these creatures depict the priests who carry the Ark of the Covenant. (The seraphim of Isaiah 6 and the living creatures of Revelation 4 have six wings.)

7.   These creatures are moved, equipped and empowered by the activity of the Spirit. The Spirit gives them life.

8.   The appearance of these angelic beings is like fire. They burn as they stand in the presence of everlasting burning, and they are radiantly reflecting the realm of glory in which they stand.

9.   Their movement is described like lightning going back and forth. Light travels at 186,000 miles per second. These creatures demonstrate an immediacy to carry the decree of YHWH. Lightning proceeds from the very being of God. There is power that emanates from God. It is within that manifestation of power that these creatures move and carry out God's decrees.

   And from the **throne proceeded lightnings,** *thunderings, and voices. Seven lamps of fire were burning before the throne, which are the seven Spirits of God. (Revelation 4:5, emphasis added)*

10.   The movements of the wings reflect the voice of the Lord like thunder and like the sound of many rushing waters.

F.   These cherubim, or guardians of the glory, stand in the realm of fire, which is the realm of the jealousy of God. Therefore, their appearance is like burning coals as they glow with the same fire and brightness as the cloud does. This fire produces zeal for the beauty of Jesus. Ezekiel had this zeal imparted to him.

*As for the likeness of the living creatures, **their appearance was like burning coals of fire,** like the appearance of torches going back and forth among the living creatures. The fire was bright, and out of the fire went lightning. And the living creatures ran back and forth, in appearance like a flash of lightning. (Ezekiel 1:13–14, emphasis added)*

*For the LORD your God is a consuming fire, **a jealous God.** (Deuteronomy 4:24, emphasis added)*

*Who makes His angels spirits, **His ministers** (angels) **a flame of fire.** (Psalm 104:4, emphasis and parenthetical comment added)*

*So the Spirit lifted me up and took me away, and I went in bitterness, **in the heat of my spirit** (Ezekiel had an impartation of the zeal for the glory of YHWH); but the hand of the LORD was strong upon me. (Ezekiel 3:14, emphasis and parenthetical comment added)*

V.   THE WHEELS (1:15–21)

A.   There is a wheel next to each living creature.

B.   In this theophany, we see the reality that the Ark of the Covenant represents, which is the throne and the presence of God.

C.   The wheels speak of the **dynamic reality and movement** of the government of God. Here we see that God's government is active and able to move across the nations of the earth.

D.   The wheels also show us that though God is transcendent, that He has the ability to be near in the most imminent way. We see His jealous desire to be with His people even in the midst of judgment. He leaves the temple and comes to the captives in prison to make it clear that He desires to be with them. This reality can easily be forgotten in an hour of crisis.

E.   The centerpiece of God's eternal purpose is for Jesus to come back to fully establish His Kingdom-rule over all the earth as He joins the heavenly and earthly realms together. God's purpose has always been to live together with His people in this way.

F.   The wheels show us the interaction of the throne of God with the earth.

*In the year that King Uzziah died, I saw the Lord sitting on **a throne, high and lifted up,** (heavenly) and the train of His **robe filled the temple** (earthly). (Isaiah 6:1, emphasis and parenthetical comments added)*

*Thus says the LORD: **"Heaven** is My throne, and **earth** is My footstool. Where is the house that you will build Me? And where is the place of My rest?" (Isaiah 66:1, emphasis added)*

G.   The wheels are related to the earthly dimensions of the glory of God. The glory of Jesus, as seen here by the river of Chebar, returns to the temple at the end of the book of Ezekiel with its heavenly and earthly dimensions (the soles of His feet).

*Afterward he brought me to the gate, the gate that faces toward the east. And behold, **the glory of the God of Israel** came from the way of the east. **His voice was like the sound of many waters;** and **the earth shone with His glory.** It was like the appearance of the vision, which I saw—like the vision, which I saw when I came to destroy the city. The visions were like the vision which I saw by the River Chebar; and I fell on my face. **And the glory of the LORD came into the temple** by way of the gate which faces toward the east. The Spirit lifted me up and brought me into the inner court; and behold, **the glory of the LORD filled the temple.** Then I heard Him speaking to me from the temple, while a man stood beside me. And He said to me, "Son of man, **this is the place of My throne** and **the place of the soles of My feet,** where I will dwell in the midst of the children of Israel forever. No more shall the house of Israel defile My holy name, they nor their kings, by their harlotry or with the carcasses of their kings on their high places." (Ezekiel 43:1–7, emphasis added)*

VI.   THE SAPPHIRE EXPANSE (1:22–25)

A.   I believe that the sapphire expanse is the same as the sea of glass mentioned in the Apostle's encounter in Revelation 4. John received a view of the throne from Heaven's perspective, while Ezekiel had a view of the throne from an earthly perspective below the sea of glass (Ezekiel 1:22).

B.   The crystal pavement that John saw in the New Testament is mentioned two times in the Old Testament, and John would have been very familiar with these references. It was first mentioned by Moses in Exodus 24:10. The second and only other man who saw and recorded it in Scripture was Ezekiel (1:22). When you put Ezekiel 1:22 with Exodus 24:10 and these together with Revelation 4:6 and Revelation 15:2, there are a number of overlapping features in each description that tie them all together.

C.   The sapphire expanse is a realm that we can encounter like the Apostle John, Ezekiel, Moses and Aaron. I believe it to be realm of revelation of the knowledge of God.

*Then **Moses went up,** also **Aaron, Nadab, and Abihu,** and **seventy of the elders of Israel,** and they **saw the God of Israel.** And there was **under His feet** as it were a **paved work of sapphire stone,** and it was like the very heavens in its clarity. (Exodus 24:9–10, emphasis added)*

*The **likeness of the firmament** above the heads of the living creatures was **like the color of an awesome crystal,** stretched out over their heads. (Ezekiel 1:22, emphasis added)*

D.   The sapphire expanse is like a platform that is connected to the throne of God, carrying and supporting it. The throne of the Son and the throne of the Father are positioned on this expanse (Ezekiel 1:26; Revelation 4:2–8).

VII.   THE SAPPHIRE THRONE (1:26)

A.   The throne of God is the center of government. All of God's highest purposes are exercised from His throne. Ezekiel saw the place of authority and the Person on the throne who is the source of all authority. John saw One on a throne (the Father), but Ezekiel saw One like a Man, the Second Person of the Trinity, who someday will be seated as a human being upon the throne of His Father. The fact that a human is sitting on the throne of God is absolutely unthinkable.

*In the year that King Uzziah died, **I saw the Lord sitting on a throne, high and lifted up** (heavenly dimension), and the train of His robe filled the temple (earthly dimension). Above it stood seraphim; each one had six wings: with two he covered his face, with two he covered his feet, and with two he flew. (Isaiah 6:1–2, emphasis and parenthetical comments added)*

*I watched till thrones were put in place, **and the Ancient of Days was seated;** His garment was white as snow, and the hair of His head was like pure wool. **His throne was a fiery flame,** its wheels a burning fire; **a fiery stream issued and came forth from before Him.** A thousand thousands ministered to Him; ten thousand times ten thousand stood before Him. The court was seated, and the books were opened. (Daniel 7:9–10, emphasis added)*

VIII. THE SON OF MAN (1:27)

A. This Man is seen above the throne, or sitting on the throne of God. The fact that He is sitting speaks of the fact that He is at rest, unmoved and unshaken by the trouble on the earth. It speaks of His sovereign leadership over the globe.

B. I believe the Holy Spirit showed Ezekiel that the full reality of God's dealings with Israel will not take place until a Man literally sits on the throne of God, which would not happen until Christ ascended on high.

C. The Man on the throne is surrounded by blinding radiance, jealousy and tenderness.

*Also from the **appearance of His waist and upward** I saw, as it were, **the color of amber with the appearance of fire all around within it;** and from the appearance of **His waist and downward I saw, as it were, the appearance of fire with brightness all around.** (Ezekiel 1:27, emphasis added)*

IX. THE GLORY OF THE SON OF MAN

*Like the **appearance of a rainbow in a cloud on a rainy day,** so was the appearance **of the brightness all around it.** This was the appearance of the likeness of the glory of the Lord. (Ezekiel 1:28, emphasis added)*

A. The Man above the throne is clothed with a bright radiance that looks like a rainbow. This speaks of Christ's enduring mercy, reminding us that in the midst of His administration of God's judgments He is also reflecting God's mercy. The same is true in the book of Revelation where we see One as a Lamb slain releasing the judgments of God. The Lamb reminds us of God's love and zeal on the cross. It is the same passion that was manifested on the cross that is manifested in the release of both His temporal and eternal judgments, as these are statements of His commitment to all that is called love and God.

B.   Just like in the book of Revelation we see the Lamb of God (the Man) loose the seals, Ezekiel 1 shows us that at the end of the age, the Son of Man will be navigating the divine storm of God's violent and furious whirlwind, releasing the judgments of God upon the nations of the earth.

*Behold, **a whirlwind of the Lord** has gone forth in **fury—a violent whirlwind!** It will fall violently on the head of the wicked. The anger of the Lord will not turn back **until He has executed and performed the thoughts of His heart. In the latter days you will understand it perfectly.** (Jeremiah 23:19–20, emphasis added)*

*But I will kindle a fire in the wall of Rabbah, and it shall devour its palaces, amid shouting in the day of battle, and a tempest in **the day of the whirlwind** (the day of the Lord). (Amos 1:14, emphasis and parenthetical comment added)*

Session Thirteen: God's Wisdom and Power—The Brilliance of His Leadership and Administration

I. OVERVIEW

*To me, who am less than the least of all the saints, this grace was given, that I should preach among the Gentiles the unsearchable riches of Christ, and to make all see what is **the fellowship of the mystery, which from the beginning of the ages has been hidden in God** who created all things through Jesus Christ; to the intent that now **the manifold wisdom of God might be made known by the church to the principalities and powers in the heavenly places,** according to the eternal purpose which He accomplished in Christ Jesus our Lord, in whom we have boldness and access with confidence through faith in Him. (Ephesians 3:8–12, emphasis added)*

A. The idea of the mystery of God speaks of the place within Him that is in accordance with the longings and the desires of His heart. The apostolic mystery is more than a theological treatise; it is an expression of the heart God. The mysteries of God are an invitation into communion with the Godhead.

B. There are many dimensions to the mystery of God, but there are four main components that are highlighted in the Word of God. There is a mystery or plan in God's heart, which He ordained before the foundations of the earth. I believe that this plan was the holy motivation behind the execution of the Genesis 1 covenant.

*But we speak the wisdom of God in a mystery, **the hidden wisdom** which God ordained before the ages for our glory . . . (1 Corinthians 2:7, emphasis added)*

C. The divine strategy (human history) is the way that God unfolds hidden information that binds our hearts to Him and enlarges us in love.

D.   This hidden plan, or blueprint, necessitated the Second Person of the Trinity becoming a man, paying the price for sin, rising from the dead, then being seated back at the right hand of God the Father before this hidden plan would be declared to humanity (the redeemed). God gave the mystery to the apostles who recorded it in the written Word of God, and it was passed down through the generations.

. . . Which in other ages was not made known to the sons of men, as it has now been revealed by the Spirit to His holy apostles and prophets . . . (Ephesians 3:5)

E.   Not until the Christ was revealed in the flesh and declared the mystery with His own mouth would the apostles know the mystery of God.

*No one has seen God at any time. The only begotten Son, **who is in the bosom of the Father, He has declared Him.** (John 1:18, emphasis added)*

F.   The unfolding of human history, as understood according to the divine mystery, impacts us and changes our emotional chemistry. God devised a plan that causes us to grow in experiencing the romance of the Gospel as He unfolds it to our hearts.

*But we speak the wisdom of God in a mystery, the hidden wisdom **which God ordained before the ages for our glory** . . . (1 Corinthians 2:7, emphasis added)*

G.   The mystery of the Gospel reveals God's plan, His power, and His Personhood. The revelation of the mystery is about the splendor of His majesty, **the greatness of His power and the brilliance of His wisdom.**

H.   The divine blueprints are called mysteries because they were hidden in the heart of God until the Second Person of the Trinity became a Man and declared it to us from His own mouth. Jesus had to be the first One to declare the mystery. The Father would not give it (that is, His own heart) or delegate it to anyone else. This mystery was locked up in the very heart of the Father Himself. Only the One who eternally dwells in the heart of God was able to faithfully declare the heart of God.

I.   God has now made the mystery plain to us by revealing it to the apostles and prophets who recorded the information in the scripture for us.

J.   God wants the whole Church to make known the mystery. He has desired this throughout church history; but especially at the end of the age, the Lord wants the Church to encounter, to walk out and to proclaim the mystery. The angels are filled with holy curiosity, longing to look into God's plan. They will gain their insight as God empowers the Church to walk out the mystery of God.

*. . . But in the days of the sounding of the seventh angel, when he is about to sound, the **mystery of God would be finished** (faithfully declared in the earth), as He declared to His servants the prophets. (Revelation 10:7, emphasis and parenthetical comment added)*

And one cried to another and said: "Holy, holy, holy is the L<small>ORD</small> of hosts; the whole earth is full of His glory!" (Isaiah 6:3)

***Of this salvation** (mystery) **the prophets have inquired and searched carefully,** who prophesied of the grace that would come to you, **searching what, or what manner of time,** the Spirit of Christ who was in them was indicating when He testified beforehand **the sufferings of Christ and the glories that would follow** (the unfolding of the mystery). **To them it was revealed that, not to themselves,** but to us they were ministering **the things which now have been reported** to you through those who have preached the gospel to you by the Holy Spirit sent from heaven— **things which angels desire to look into.** (1 Peter 1:10–12, emphasis and parenthetical comments added)*

*. . . To the intent that **now the manifold wisdom of God might be made known by the church to the principalities and powers in the heavenly places,** according to the eternal purpose which He accomplished in Christ Jesus our Lord... (Ephesians 3:10–11, emphasis added)*

II.   THE WISDOM REVEALED IN THE MYSTERY PRODUCES CONFIDENCE IN THE FUTURE

*. . . In whom we have **boldness and access with confidence** through faith in Him. Therefore I ask that you **do not lose heart at my tribulations** for you, which is your glory. (Ephesians 3:12–13, emphasis added)*

A.   The Father has a plan, which He conceived in Himself. This plan was rooted and grounded in the good pleasure of God. It reveals the unsearchable riches of Christ.

B. The revelation of the mystery of eternity produces confidence and boldness instead of timidity and shame because in it we can see the determined will of God and His zeal to bring them to the end. We can see the Father's passion in the very plan itself.

*I know that You can do everything, and that **no purpose of Yours can be withheld** from You. (Job 42:2, emphasis added)*

C. The wisdom of God has to do with God's skill to carry out His own plan. It speaks of the brilliance of His leadership. He is the only wise God, and through His administration, not one of His plans or purposes is thwarted.

Oh, the depth of the riches both of the wisdom and knowledge of God! *How unsearchable are His judgments and His ways past finding out! "For who has known the mind of the LORD? Or who has become His counselor?" "Or who has first given to Him and it shall be repaid to him?" For of Him and through Him and to Him are all things, to whom be glory forever. Amen. (Romans 11:33–36, emphasis added)*

D. God wants us to know that He devised a plan for His people rooted in His passion and in His pleasure. This eternal purpose is profoundly rooted in His gladness and kindness toward His Son and the very people who would be in the Son's embrace.

To them God willed *to make known what are **the riches of the glory of this mystery** among the Gentiles: which is Christ in you, the hope of glory. (Colossians 1:27, emphasis added)*

*. . . Having **predestined us to adoption as sons by Jesus Christ to Himself,** according to the **good pleasure of His will** . . . (Ephesians 1:5, emphasis added)*

*. . . Having made known to us the **mystery of His will,** according to **His good pleasure** which He purposed in Himself . . . (Ephesians 1:9, emphasis added)*

III. THE MYSTERY: VOLUNTARY LOVERS IN GOD'S EMBRACE FOREVER

*. . . That in the dispensation of the fullness of the times He might gather together in one all things in Christ, both which are **in heaven** and which are **on earth**—in Him. (Ephesians 1:10, emphasis added)*

A.   The centerpiece of God's eternal purpose is for Jesus to come back to fully establish His Kingdom-rule over all the earth as He joins the heavenly and earthly realms together. God's purpose has always been to live together with His people in this way. This is the interpretive key to understanding the Gospel.

B.   The heavens speak of the spiritual realm. The earth speaks of the natural realm. The real trouble is in the natural realm because it is where all sorts of evil passions and temptations find their expression. God, in His brilliance, determined that He would reconcile Heaven and Earth and out of that context He would bring forth voluntary lovers.

C.   This plan would be brought forth with difficulty, but the Father was determined to bring out of creation voluntary lovers as an inheritance for His Son.

D.   God determined not to "make" something happen. **It takes the very wisdom of God (manifold) to exercise the brilliance of His leadership to have voluntary lovers for His Son.** He wants voluntary lovers because God would use the magnificence of His manifold wisdom without violating the human will.

E.   The grace of God has touched our hearts (invited us), but we have to say, "Yes!" to walk in the invitation of God. God will touch us with His power and influence, but He will not violate the dignity of the human spirit to make free choices. Somewhere in the struggle of temptations, the pleasure of sin, our not-yet-renewed minds, demonic activity and oppression, God will exercise the brilliance of His leadership—but we must say "yes" by our own choice to become voluntary lovers out of the human race called the Body of Christ.

F.   The Father says, "Voluntary lovers is what I have ordained for You. At the end of natural history, there will be a company of people that chose You because they wanted You, because they saw You wanted them."

> *. . . That at the name of Jesus **every knee should bow,** of those in heaven, and of those on earth, and of those under the earth, and **that every tongue should confess** that Jesus Christ is Lord, to the glory of God the Father. (Philippians 2:10–11, emphasis added)*

> *Your people shall be **volunteers in the day of Your power;** in the beauties of holiness, from the womb of the morning, You have the dew of Your youth. (Psalm 110:3, emphasis added)*

G.   Voluntary lovers are the inheritance of Christ Jesus (Ephesians 1:17–19). The unfolding of this great mystery is the merging of Heaven and Earth, the natural and the spiritual realms. God created the natural realm where humanity cannot see God face to face. He allowed sin to dwell and reign in our members, let the devil attack us and allowed our minds to be darkened in their understanding because of sin.

H.   God's infinite wisdom is expressed in the context of the natural realm and the dynamic of real choices. As many have said "Yes!" He has led them to the Son and will present them to Him in the end.

I.   The choice to say "No!" is as real as the choice to say "Yes!" Eternal damnation and the Lake of Fire are real. The Lake of Fire will have billions of human beings in it because they really said "No!" to the infinitely kind God in His awesome offer and blueprints to have voluntary lovers at the end of the age.

J.   The human spirit is so dignified because we have the power to make life and death choices that matter in time and Eternity. The reality of choice dignifies love.

IV.   ETERNITY: THE CONSUMMATION OF ALL PERFECTION

A.   The blueprints culminate with a Bride cleansed and enthroned and brought to full beauty in the embrace of Christ Jesus by her own choice and by His choice.

B.   The dynamic of voluntary love is what makes life so hard, but that is also what makes life so glorious when we choose Him. The temptations and the choices are real, making the journey of redemption difficult and hard, therefore the choice of love is real, and it matters to God.

C.   Every movement in our spirits toward Him matters to Him even though we might stumble in the outworking of our intentions. The very intention matters to God. The very movement of our heart to say "Yes!" to Him, even though we come up short in walking it out, matters in this age as well as the age to come.

> ***You have ravished My heart,*** *My sister, My spouse;* ***You have ravished My heart** **with one look of your eyes,*** *with one link of your necklace (Song of Solomon 4:9, emphasis added)*

D.   The Mystery of Eternity: The hidden blueprints started from eternity and were hidden in the heart of God to give Jesus an inheritance. Jesus' inheritance is a Bride reigning and ruling like Him, who will look like Him, talk like Him, love like Him, feel like Him, think like Him and have authority like Him.

V.   THE WISDOM AND POWER OF GOD

*Now to the King eternal, immortal, invisible, **to God who alone is wise,** be honor and glory forever and ever. Amen. (1 Timothy 1:17, emphasis added)*

A.   *Wisdom, among other things, is the ability to devise perfect ends and to achieve those ends by the most perfect means. It sees the end from the beginning, so there can be no need to guess or conjecture. Wisdom sees everything in focus, each in proper relation to all, and is thus able to work toward predestined goals with flawless precision.*[1]

B.   God, in His wisdom, sees the end from the beginning and carries out His plans, leading the redeemed into His eternal purpose.

***Declaring the end from the beginning,** and from ancient times things that are not yet done, saying, **"My counsel shall stand, and I will do all My pleasure** . . ." (Isaiah 46:10, emphasis added)*

C.   God's wisdom is His essence and it is something He possesses (Proverbs 8:22–31; 1 Corinthians 1). The wisdom of God consists of the ability to know what to do in all circumstances to bring about a desired end, knowing what action will bring about what results in light of the big picture. He is able to act with good and pure intent (James 3) for the cause of truth, righteousness, love and humility.

---

1   Tozer, A.W. *The Knowledge of the Holy* (San Francisco: HarperSanFrancisco, 1961), p. 60.

For the message of the cross is foolishness to those who are perishing, but to us who are being saved it is the power of God. For it is written: "I will destroy the wisdom of the wise, and bring to nothing the understanding of the prudent." Where is the wise? Where is the scribe? Where is the disputer of this age? Has not God made foolish the wisdom of this world? **For since, in the wisdom of God, the world through wisdom did not know God, it pleased God through the foolishness of the message preached to save those who believe.** *For Jews request a sign, and Greeks seek after wisdom; but we preach Christ crucified, to the Jews a stumbling block and to the Greeks foolishness, but to those who are called, both Jews and Greeks,* **Christ the power of God and the wisdom of God.** *Because the foolishness of God is wiser than men, and the weakness of God is stronger than men. For you see your calling, brethren, that not many wise according to the flesh, not many mighty, not many noble, are called. But God has chosen the foolish things of the world to put to shame the wise, and God has chosen the weak things of the world to put to shame the things which are mighty; and the base things of the world and the things which are despised God has chosen, and the things which are not, to bring to nothing the things that are, that no flesh should glory in His presence.* **But of Him you are in Christ Jesus, who became for us wisdom from God—and righteousness and sanctification and redemption**—*that, as it is written, "He who glories, let him glory in the* LORD. *(1 Corinthians 1:18–31, emphasis added)*

D.   God imparts His wisdom to His people (James 3:13–17, Proverbs). There are eight components of the wisdom that is from above (James 3:17).

    1.   Pure

    2.   Peaceable

    3.   Gentle

    4.   Willing to yield

    5.   Full of mercy

    6.   Good fruits

    7.   Impartial

    8.   Sincere

*And Solomon said: "You have shown great mercy to Your servant David my father, because he walked before You in truth, in righteousness, and in uprightness of heart with You; You have continued this great kindness for him, and You have given him a son to sit on his throne, as it is this day. Now, O Lord my God, You have made Your servant king instead of my father David, but I am a little child; I do not know how to go out or come in. And Your servant is in the midst of Your people whom You have chosen, a great people, too numerous to be numbered or counted. **Therefore give to Your servant an understanding heart to judge Your people, that I may discern between good and evil. For who is able to judge this great people of Yours?"***

*The speech pleased the Lord, that Solomon had asked this thing. Then God said to him: "Because you have asked this thing, and have not asked long life for yourself, nor have asked riches for yourself, nor have asked the life of your enemies, but have asked for yourself understanding to discern justice, behold, I have done according to your words; see, **I have given you a wise and understanding heart,** so that there has not been anyone like you before you, nor shall any like you arise after you." (1 Kings 3:6–12, emphasis added)*

And God gave Solomon wisdom and exceedingly great understanding, and largeness of heart like the sand on the seashore. Thus Solomon's wisdom excelled the wisdom of all the men of the East and all the wisdom of Egypt. For he was wiser than all men—than Ethan the Ezrahite, and Heman, Chalcol, and Darda, the sons of Mahol; and his fame was in all the surrounding nations. He spoke three thousand proverbs, and his songs were one thousand and five. Also he spoke of trees, from the cedar tree of Lebanon even to the hyssop that springs out of the wall; he spoke also of animals, of birds, of creeping things, and of fish. And men of all nations, from all the kings of the earth who had heard of his wisdom, came to hear the wisdom of Solomon. (1 Kings 4:29–34)

E.   By wisdom God leads the affairs of men.

*I watched till thrones were put in place, and the Ancient of Days was seated; His garment was white as snow, and **the hair of His head was like pure wool.** His throne was a fiery flame, its wheels a burning fire . . . (Daniel 7:9, emphasis added)*

His head and hair were white like wool, as white as snow, and His eyes like a flame of fire . . . (Revelation 1:14, emphasis added)

Blessed be the name of God forever and ever, for wisdom and might are His. And He changes the times and the seasons; He removes kings and raises up kings; He gives wisdom to the wise and knowledge to those who have understanding. (Daniel 2:20–21, emphasis added)

F.   His power is related to three things:

1.   Salvation and the unfolding of the plan of redemption

For I am not ashamed of the gospel of Christ, for it is the power of God to salvation for everyone who believes, for the Jew first and also for the Greek. For in it the righteousness of God is revealed from faith to faith; as it is written, "The just shall live by faith." (Romans 1:16–17, emphasis added)

2.   Sanctification and justificiation

. . . And what is the exceeding greatness of His power toward us who believe, according to the working of His mighty power which He worked in Christ when He raised Him from the dead and seated Him at His right hand in the heavenly places, far above all principality and power and might and dominion, and every name that is named, not only in this age but also in that which is to come. (Ephesians 1:19–21, emphasis added)

3.   He imparts His power to His redeemed

But you shall receive power when the Holy Spirit has come upon you; and you shall be witnesses to Me in Jerusalem, and in all Judea and Samaria, and to the end of the earth. (Acts 1:8, emphasis added)

G.   The Covenant of the Lord (Isaiah 59:21): The fullness of God's purpose will be established by the Word and the Spirit. The Father gave Jesus, in His humanity, the fullness of the Spirit and the Word by which He would execute the plan of God in the earth.

H. The power of the Spirit moves in response to the Word of God. It is interesting to note that the two premiere weapons given to Jesus by way of covenant are:

1. The Spirit

2. The Word (the sharp sword out of His mouth)

Behold! **My Servant** *whom I uphold, My Elect One in whom My soul delights!* **I have put My Spirit upon Him;** *He will bring forth* **justice** *to the Gentiles. (Isaiah 42:1, emphasis added)*

"As for Me," says the Lord, *"this is My covenant with them:* **My Spirit who is upon you, and My words which I have put in your mouth,** *shall not depart from your mouth, nor from the mouth of your descendants, nor from the mouth of your descendants' descendants," says the* Lord, *"from this time and forevermore." (Isaiah 59:21, emphasis added)*

I. The Spirit of God moves when there is agreement with the Word of God. There are three ways the we enter into agreement with the Word, and Jesus is the embodiment of that full agreement in His humanity:

1. Prayer

2. Preaching

3. Practice (obedience)

J. It is my opinion that these three realities make up what the Scripture calls abiding. The Scripture says that when we abide in the Word we will be able to declare things and watch Heaven respond. This truth has been limited mostly to bringing about domestic tranquility and stability; but in the Scripture, this measure of authority to move in God's creative power through a word is seen in the context of furthering the purposes of God.

If you abide in Me, and My words abide in you, you will ask what you desire, and it shall be done for you. (John 15:7)

But on this one will I look: *on him who is poor and of a contrite spirit, and* **who trembles at My word.** *(Isaiah 66:2, emphasis added)*

Now acquaint yourself with Him, and be at peace; thereby good will come to you. Receive, please, instruction from His mouth, and lay up His words in your heart. If you return to the Almighty, you will be built up; you will remove iniquity far from your tents. Then you will lay your gold in the dust, and the gold of Ophir among the stones of the brooks. Yes, the Almighty will be your gold and your precious silver; for then you will have your delight in the Almighty, and lift up your face to God. You will make your prayer to Him, He will hear you, and you will pay your vows. You will also declare a thing, and it will be established for you; so light will shine on your ways. (Job 22:21–28, emphasis added)

1. Elijah stopped the rain.

    *And Elijah the Tishbite, of the inhabitants of Gilead, said to Ahab, "As the LORD God of Israel lives, before whom I stand, there shall not be dew nor rain these years, **except at my word.**" (1 Kings 17:1, emphasis added)*

    *These (two witnesses) **have power to shut heaven, so that no rain falls** in the days of their prophecy . . . (Revelation 11:6, emphasis and parenthetical comment added)*

2. Paul struck a man with blindness through a word.

    *"And now, indeed, **the hand of the Lord is upon you, and you shall be blind,** not seeing the sun for a time." And **immediately a dark mist fell on him,** and he went around seeking someone to lead him by the hand. (Acts 13:11, emphasis added)*

3. Jesus withered a fig tree through a word.

    *And seeing a fig tree by the road, He came to it and found nothing on it but leaves, and **said to it, "Let no fruit grow on you ever again." Immediately the fig tree withered away.** (Matthew 21:19, emphasis added)*

4. Men fell before the Son of God at a word.

    *Now **when He said** to them, "I am He," **they drew back and fell to the ground.** (John 18:6, emphasis added)*

5. Men were struck with fire through a word.

    *So Elijah answered and **said to the captain of fifty, "If I am a man of God, then let fire come down from heaven and consume you and your fifty men." And fire came down from heaven and consumed him and his fifty.** (2 Kings 1:10, emphasis added)*

*And if anyone wants to harm them, **fire proceeds from their mouth and devours their enemies.** And if anyone wants to harm them, he must be killed in this manner. (Revelation 11:5, emphasis added)*

6.   Death occurred through a word.

*Then Peter said to her, "How is it that you have agreed together to test the Spirit of the Lord? **Look, the feet of those who have buried your husband are at the door, and they will carry you out." Then immediately she fell down at his feet and breathed her last.** And the young men came in and found her dead, and carrying her out, buried her by her husband. (Acts 5:9–10, emphasis added)*

7.   Sicknesses were removed through a word.

*This man heard Paul speaking. Paul, observing him intently and seeing that he had faith to be healed, said with a loud voice, **"Stand up straight on your feet!"** And he leaped and walked. (Acts 14:9–10, emphasis added)*

8.   Armies were resisted through a word.

*So when the Syrians came down to him, Elisha prayed to the LORD, and said, **"Strike this people, I pray, with blindness." And He struck them with blindness according to the word of Elisha.** (2 Kings 6:18, emphasis added)*

*And if anyone wants to harm them, **fire proceeds from their mouth and devours their enemies.** And if anyone wants to harm them, he must be killed in this manner. (Revelation 11:5, emphasis added)*

9.   Plagues were released through a word.

*. . . And they have power over waters to turn them to blood, and to strike the earth with all plagues, **as often as they desire.** (Revelation 11:6, emphasis added)*

K.   The Son of God will strike the earth with the rod of His mouth. The rod of His mouth speaks of prophetic, intercessory and worship decrees. Jesus will operate in the fullness of those things that are seen as tokens in the Word of God. During His First Coming, His priestly life was manifested in the natural in weakness, yet with the fullness of power in the realm of the Spirit (Colossians 2:15); but at the end of the age, His priestly ministry will be manifested in full power in the natural (Isaiah 11:4) and in the fullness of power in the realm of the Spirit (Revelation 20:1–3).

> *. . . **He shall strike the earth with the rod of His mouth,** and **with the breath of His lips** He shall **slay the wicked.** (Isaiah 11:4, emphasis added)*

L.   During the Armageddon Campaign, Jesus will slay the nations with the word of His mouth. He will speak the word and mountains will split, plagues and pestilences will be released, hundred pound hailstones, earthquakes, confusion, madness, blindness, bloodshed, flooding, fire and brimstone will be released at His word.

> *In that day," says the LORD, "I will **strike every horse with confusion,** and its **rider with madness;** I will open My eyes on the house of Judah, and **will strike every horse of the peoples with blindness."** (Zechariah 12:4, emphasis added)*

> *And this shall be the plague with which the LORD will strike all the people who fought against Jerusalem: Their flesh shall dissolve while they stand on their feet, their eyes shall dissolve in their sockets, and their tongues shall dissolve in their mouths. It shall come to pass in that day that a great panic from the LORD will be among them. Everyone will seize the hand of his neighbor, and raise his hand against his neighbor's hand . . . (Zechariah 14:12–13)*

> *And I will bring him to judgment with pestilence and bloodshed; I will rain down on him, on his troops, and on the many peoples who are with him, flooding rain, great hailstones, fire, and brimstone. (Ezekiel 38:22)*

Session Fourteen: And He Was Given Dominion

I. GOD'S DOMINION

A. The dominion of God is related to the span of His divine authority and the splendor of His majesty. God is the sovereign ruler of all creation in Heaven and on Earth.

B. The dominion of God is alluded to by the many references to His throne in the Word of God. The throne of God is the seat of government over all that exits; it is from where the King rules His kingdom. When we look at the throne of God, we gain insight into His government.

C. Since there is none greater than God, He derives His authority from Himself. No one has established God or put Him into place but God Himself.

D. *It is a dominion that originally resides in his nature, not derived from any by birth or commission; He alone prepared it. He is the sole cause of His own kingdom; his authority therefore is unbounded, as infinite as his nature: none can set laws to him, because none but himself prepared his throne for him.*[1]

II. THE THRONE ROOM OF HEAVEN

A. There is a divine invitation for us to peer into the glorious throne of God, as we are seated all together in heavenly places in Christ Jesus. There is a door standing open in heaven; it is a door of revelation that we can enter into by Divine escort.

B. The throne of God is the power, dominion and sovereign majesty revealed.

C. On the throne is One who is filled with splendor and beauty (jasper, sardius, emerald rainbow). The One on the throne is seen as sitting, referring to the fact that He is resting and reigning.

---

1 Charnock, Stephen. *The Existence and Attributes of God, Volume 2* (Grand Rapids: Baker Books, 2005), p. 360.

D. Around the throne of God are seated twenty-four elders. It is my opinion that these are redeemed humans who partake at the very core of God's governmental leadership team. The beauty of God adorns the elders. They are enthroned, clothed and crowned.

E. There is lightning, thundering and voices that break forth from God's throne.

F. The Seven Spirits are before the throne:

1. The Spirit of YHWH

2. The Spirit of Wisdom

3. The Spirit of Understanding

4. The Spirit of Counsel

5. The Spirit of Strength

6. The Spirit of Knowledge

7. The Spirit of the Fear of YHWH

G. Around the throne there is a sea of glass like crystal and four living creatures (seraphim).

H. *A throne is proper to royalty, the seat of majesty in its Excellency, and the place where the deepest respect and homage of subjects is paid, and their petitions presented. That the throne of God is in the heavens, that there he sits as Sovereign, is the opinion of all that acknowledge a God; when they stand in need of His authority to assist them, their eyes are lifted up, and their heads stretched out to heaven; so his Son Christ prayer; he "lifted up his eyes to heaven," as the place where his Father sat in majesty, as the most adorable object (John xvii. 1).*[2]

I. The dominion of God is:

---

2   Charnock, Stephen. *The Existence and Attributes of God, Volume 2* (Grand Rapids: Baker Books, 2005), p. 360.

1.   Glorious—it is filled with beauty and splendor (the beauty realm).

2.   Supreme—the rule of God is above all (Isaiah 6:1).

3.   Vast—the rule of God is infinitely far-reaching (Isaiah 9:7).

4.   Eternal—the domain of the King will know no end (Hebrews 12:28).

III.   THE SEVENFOLD BEAUTY OF JESUS (HIS HUMAN PERSONALITY AND ABILITIES)

*Then God said, "Let Us make man in Our image, according to Our likeness; **let them have dominion** over the fish of the sea, over the birds of the air, and over the cattle, over all the earth and over every creeping thing that creeps on the earth." So God created man in His own image; in the image of God He created him; male and female He created them. Then God blessed them, and God said to them, "Be fruitful and multiply; fill the earth and subdue it; **have dominion** over the fish of the sea, over the birds of the air, and over every living thing that moves on the earth." (Genesis 1:26–28, emphasis added)*

*When I consider Your heavens, the work of Your fingers, the moon and the stars, which You have ordained, what is man that You are mindful of him, and the son of man that You visit him? For You have made him a little lower than the angels, and **You have crowned him with glory and honor. You have made him to have dominion over the works of Your hands;** You have put all things under his feet, all sheep and oxen—even the beasts of the field, the birds of the air, and the fish of the sea that pass through the paths of the seas. (Psalm 8:3–8, emphasis added)*

*I was watching in the night visions, and behold, One like the Son of Man, coming with the clouds of heaven! He came to the Ancient of Days, and they brought Him near before Him. **Then to Him was given dominion** and glory and a kingdom, that all peoples, nations, and languages should serve Him. His dominion is an everlasting dominion, which shall not pass away, and His kingdom the one which shall not be destroyed. (Daniel 7:13–14, emphasis added)*

A.   **Power** (political): Jesus will receive governmental leadership and power over the nations of the earth when He returns. The kingdoms of this world will become the kingdoms of God and His Christ.

B.   **Riches** (financial): All the wealth of the nations will be transferred to Jesus' leadership (Haggai 2:8). God will give Jesus the power to make wealth (see the story of the Magi in Luke 2; 1 Kings 10).

C.   **Wisdom** (intellectual): Jesus will be entrusted with the divine administration. Jesus' wisdom will determine the global plan for all areas including agriculture, environment, economy, education, family life, social infrastructure. He will have the skill necessary to establish the leadership of the Godhead in the earth.

D.   **Strength** (emotional): Jesus will have strength in His inner man (Ephesians 3:16) unto continuing steadfastly in the fruits of the Spirit (kindness, mercy, goodness, etc.). He will have sustaining grace to contend against all resistance until the full establishing and breakthrough of God's plan and purpose. His mercy endures over all our failure and resistance. Jesus shall rebuke many nations (Isaiah 2:4) yet will not be stressed out with weariness, thus losing focus, wavering in kindness, forgetting details, etc. He will not get weary, distracted, bitter or impatient with us. He has the strength to stand in the anointing (Daniel 10:19).

E.   **Honor** (relational): The saints will greatly esteem and value Jesus and thus respond to Him with affectionate loyalty (personal devotion) and confidence in Him.

F.   **Glory** (supernatural or spiritual): Jesus, as worldwide Emperor, will operate in the supernatural realm (anointing of the Spirit).

G.   **Blessing** (social): Jesus will have the people of all nations in full agreement and cooperation with Him (angels and people in Heaven and Earth—Ephesians 1:10). His support base and work force will be very strong. **We decree that the agreement and cooperation of the nations with the Antichrist's leadership will break down.**

IV. ESTABLISHMENT OF GOD'S FULL DOMINION PRECEDED BY MILITARY BATTLE

A. The centerpiece of God's eternal purpose is for Jesus to come back and fully establish His Kingdom-rule over all the earth as He joins the heavenly and earthly realms together. God's purpose has always been to live together with His people in this way. This is the interpretive key to understanding the End Times. Without this foundational revelation, confusion is inevitable when studying the End Times.

> *. . . Having made known to us **the mystery of His will,** according to His good pleasure which He purposed in Himself, that in the dispensation of the fullness of the times **He might gather together in one all things in Christ, both which are in heaven and which are on earth—in Him.** (Ephesians 1:9–10, emphasis added)*

B. There is a warfare dimension related to the execution of God's plan. It will not be executed without a battle. He came to defeat the enemy at the Cross, to make a public spectacle of the devil, and render powerless the realms of darkness. He will also come and engage in battle in the natural realm at the Battle of Jerusalem. The purpose of His Second Coming is to manifest the fullness of God's government on the earth, establishing His throne in Jerusalem; this will be **preceded by a military battle.**

C. Commonly, the subject of warfare is limited to a battle fought in the spirit. However, there is a battle to be fought in the natural at the Campaign of Armageddon by Christ in His humanity. There is a revelation of the mystery of Christ as the God-Man and Warrior-King. The warfare that Christ wages will be in the realm of the spirit and the realm of the natural.

D. The God-Man, who is a warrior, fights demons; but He will fight a battle in the natural with human processes, yet with supernatural activity upon it.

E. The Armageddon Campaign is **not** the colliding of two world powers like communism and democracy, or two world superpowers at war with each other, bringing the earth to the brink of destruction. At Armageddon, the nations of the earth will fight against God and His armies.

*The ten horns which you saw are ten kings who have received no kingdom as yet, but they receive authority for one hour as kings with the beast. These are of one mind, and they will give their power and authority to the beast. **These will make war with the Lamb, and the Lamb will overcome them,** for He is Lord of lords and King of kings; and those who are with Him are called, chosen, and faithful. (Revelation 17:12–14, emphasis added)*

F.   The issue of the Armageddon Campaign is Jerusalem, because Jerusalem will be where the government of Heaven and Earth will be brought together under the Father's authority.

*". . . **in that day that I will make Jerusalem a very heavy stone for all peoples;** all who would heave it away will surely be cut in pieces, though all nations of the earth are gathered against it. In that day," says the* Lord, *"I will strike every horse with confusion, and its rider with madness . . . **In that day the** Lord **will defend the inhabitants of Jerusalem** . . . It shall be in that day that **I will seek to destroy all the nations that come against Jerusalem."** (Zechariah 12:3–4, 8–9, emphasis added)*

Session Fifteen: And He Was Given Dominion, Part Two

I. THE SOVEREIGNTY OF GOD

A. *God's sovereignty is the attribute by which He rules His entire creation, and to be sovereign God must be all knowing, all powerful, and absolutely free. The reasons are these: Were there even one datum of knowledge, however small, unknown to God, His rule would break down at that point. To be Lord over all the creation, He must possess all knowledge. And were God lacking one infinitesimal modicum of power, that lack would end His reign and undo His kingdom; that one stray atom of power would belong to someone else and God would be a limited ruler and hence not sovereign.*[1]

B. God has chosen to manifest the fullness of His sovereignty in and through the Man Christ Jesus

   . . . That you keep this commandment without spot, blameless until our Lord Jesus Christ's appearing, which He will manifest in His own time, He who is the blessed and only Potentate, the King of kings and Lord of lords, who alone has immortality, dwelling in unapproachable light, whom no man has seen or can see, to whom be *honor and everlasting power. Amen. (1 Timothy 6:14–16)*

   And Jesus came and spoke to them, saying, "All authority has been given to Me in heaven and on earth." (Matthew 28:18)

II. ARMAGGEDON: THE BATTLE LEADING UP TO ESTABLISHMENT OF THE THRONE ON EARTH

And one cried to another and said: "Holy, holy, holy is the LORD of hosts; the whole earth is full of His glory!" (Isaiah 6:3, emphasis added)

*Who is this who comes from Edom, with dyed garments from Bozrah, **this One who is glorious in His apparel,** traveling in the greatness of His strength? (Isaiah 63:1, emphasis added)*

A. The primary objective of studying the Armageddon Campaign is the discovery of the beauty of Christ's personality. Studying this subject enlarges our hearts in love and fills us with wonder.

---

1   Tozer, A.W. *The Knowledge of the Holy* (San Franscisco: HarperSanFrancisco, 1961), p.108.

This is the day the Lord *has made;* **we will rejoice and be glad in it.** *(Psalm 118:24, emphasis added)*

B.   There is divine information, divine treasures, in the heart of Christ concerning the Day of His vengeance that He longs for us to know.

For the day of vengeance is in My heart, *and the year of My redeemed has come. (Isaiah 63:4, emphasis added)*

. . . That their hearts may be encouraged, being knit together in love, and attaining to all riches of the full assurance of understanding, to the knowledge of the mystery of God, both of the Father and of Christ, in whom are hidden all the treasures of wisdom and knowledge. (Colossians 2:2–3)

III.   KING OF KINGS AND LORD OF LORDS

. . . And on His head were many crowns. He had a name written that no one knew except Himself. (Revelation 19:12)

A.   The central issue of the Armageddon Campaign is the beauty of Jesus to the glory of the Father. As He comes to the earth for the final battle of natural history, He comes with many crowns. I believe that the many crowns speak of His manifold authority in both Heaven and Earth (Matthew 28:18), His reward that comes with Him (Isaiah 62:11), and that name that is above every name because of His meekness and humility (Philippians 2:9–11).

B.   The are four names of the Son of God in the Armageddon Campaign that are central to the unfolding of the beauty of the Lord:

1.   Faithful and True

2.   The Word of God (Logos)

3.   The name that no one knew except Himself (the name that is above every name)

4.   King of Kings and Lord of Lords

C.   He comes with the fullness of the Father's reward to rule and reign on the earth as King of Kings and Lord of Lords.

And He has on His robe and on His thigh a name written: KING OF KINGS AND LORD OF LORDS. (Revelation 19:16)

D. Jesus is the Logos of God. He is the full expression of God in the flesh.

. . . And His name is called The Word (Logos) *of God. (Revelation 19:13, parenthetical comment added)*

IV. NOW I SAW HEAVEN OPENED, AND BEHOLD, A WHITE HORSE

A. Jesus will fight the nations of the earth on a horse. This is because the earth is completely war-torn and devastated after all the catastrophes that hit the planet (Isaiah 24). Horses will most likely be the only way that people will get from one place to the other. After Hurricane Katrina, it took three to four days before any outside help could enter the city. The end-time landscape will require actual horses.

B. The Armageddon Campaign will be a war fought by means of natural human processes with a strong supernatural component to it.

V. AND HE WHO SAT ON HIM WAS CALLED FAITHFUL AND TRUE

A. The Second Coming of Jesus is ultimately about establishing the dominion of God on the earth. Jesus will come back and make wrong things right in every arena of life. The Armageddon Campaign reveals Christ as Faithful and True, contrary to the nature of the Antichrist who will be filled with lies and empty promises—he is the son of perdition under the full influence of the Father of lies. Revelation of the Warrior-King fills our hearts with hope because it is the revelation of the fact that He can be trusted and will **follow through on all that He promised,** to bring righteousness, salvation and vengeance (justice) (Isaiah 59:17–18).

B. God's zeal is to make wrong things right. His commitment is to end all expressions of sin, rebellion, injustice, poverty, oppression, racism, systemic injustice, corruption, etc. The ending of the Armageddon Campaign is a part of our hope in the Gospel that justice will be established in the earth.

C. At the end of the age there will be steady decline of personal, societal, national and global morality. God will put an end to it by sending His Son to establish His government in Jerusalem, which is preceded by military battle.

*But the **rest of mankind** (across the globe), who were not killed by these plagues **did not repent of the works of their hands,** that they should not **worship demons,** and idols of gold, silver, brass, stone, and wood, which can neither see nor hear nor walk. And **they did not repent** of their **murders** or their **sorceries** or their **sexual immorality** or their **thefts.** (Revelation 9:20–21, emphasis and parenthetical comment added)*

D.   Jesus will come with the authority of the Father to accomplish the task of establishing justice in the earth. The revelation of Him being Faithful and True gives us insight into His splendor, the beauty of His character and His majesty. J. Alec Motyer says, "It is a work which will display and satisfy his righteousness, save his people, repay his foes and be carried through to completion by the driving motivation of divine zeal."[2] This revelation of God's zeal and fury is what will give the Church and the poor and the oppressed of the earth assurance that justice will come to those who **entrust their lives to the leadership of Jesus.**

*Of the increase of His government and peace there will be no end, upon the throne of David and over His kingdom, **to order it and establish it with judgment and justice** from that time forward, even forever. **The zeal of the Lord of hosts will perform this.** (Isaiah 9:7, emphasis added)*

. . . Since it is a righteous thing with God to repay with tribulation those who trouble you, and to give you who are troubled rest with us when the Lord Jesus is revealed from heaven with His mighty angels, in flaming fire taking vengeance on those who do not know God, and on those who do not obey the gospel of our Lord Jesus Christ. (2 Thessalonians 1:6–8)

E.   Jesus will fight this final military battle so that He can establish justice by releasing salvation on those who have said yes to His Gospel and by releasing vengeance on those who oppose His Gospel.

*Behold! My Servant whom I uphold, My Elect One in whom My soul delights! I have put My Spirit upon Him; **He will bring forth justice to the Gentiles.** (Isaiah 42:1, emphasis added)*

*He will not fail nor be discouraged, **till He has established justice in the earth;** And the coastlands shall wait for His law. (Isaiah 42:4, emphasis added)*

---

2   Motyer, J. Alec. *The Prophecy of Isaiah: An Introduction and Commentary* (Downers Grove, IL: InterVarsity Press, 1993), p. 491.

The LORD shall go forth like a mighty man; **He shall stir up His zeal like a man of war.** *He shall cry out, yes, shout aloud;* **He shall prevail against His enemies.** *(Isaiah 42:13, emphasis added)*

Listen to Me, My people; and give ear to Me, O My nation: for law will proceed from Me, **and I will make My justice rest as a light of the peoples.** *(Isaiah 51:4, emphasis added)*

VI.   AND IN RIGHTEOUSNESS HE JUDGES AND MAKES WAR

A.   The motivations of the Son of God are filled with righteousness as He wages war against the nations of the earth. Most wars in human history were not fought with righteous motivation to establish a kingdom under the leadership of God for His glory so that all nations would serve Him.

I can of Myself do nothing. **As I hear, I judge; and My judgment is righteous,** *because* **I do not seek My own will but the will of the Father** *who sent Me. (John 5:30, emphasis added)*

B.   The Armageddon Campaign is as much a judgment against the nations as it is a war.

"A noise will come to the ends of the earth— **for the LORD has a controversy with the nations; He will plead His case with all flesh.** *He will give those who are wicked to the sword," says the LORD. (Jeremiah 25:31, emphasis added)*

I will also gather all nations, and bring them down to the Valley of Jehoshaphat; and I will enter into judgment with them there on account of My people, My heritage Israel, whom they have scattered among the nations; they have also divided up My land. (Joel 3:2)

"Let the nations be wakened, and come up to the Valley of Jehoshaphat; **for there I will sit to judge all the surrounding nations.** *Put in the sickle, for the harvest is ripe. Come, go down; for the winepress is full, the vats overflow—for their wickedness is great."* **Multitudes, multitudes in the valley of decision! For the day of the LORD is near in the valley of decision.** *(Joel 3:12–14, emphasis added)*

*I will call for a sword against Gog throughout all My mountains," says the Lord GOD. "Every man's sword will be against his brother. **And I will bring him to judgment with pestilence and bloodshed; I will rain down** on him, on his troops, and on the many peoples who are with him, **flooding rain, great hailstones, fire, and brimstone."** (Ezekiel 38:21–22, emphasis added)*

C.   Jesus is waging war against the Antichrist, of whose ability to make war the earth was in awe. He responds to the challenge of the nations of the earth and wages war.

*So they worshiped the dragon who gave authority to the beast; and they worshiped the beast, saying, "Who is like the beast? **Who is able to make war with him?"** (Revelation 13:4, emphasis added)*

*But in their place he shall honor **a god of fortresses** . . . (Daniel 11:38, emphasis added)*

VII.   HIS EYES WERE LIKE A FLAME OF FIRE

A.   The flaming eyes could speak of Christ's ability to search the hearts and minds of His people. His eyes speak of His infinite knowledge, wisdom, understanding, and discernment. (Revelation 2:18, 23). The fire in His eyes reveals the zeal that He possesses in His being for the Father and His purposes in the earth.

B.   Jesus will come with the judgment and the assessment of His Father so that the nations of the earth would honor the Son and so honor the Father.

*Then Jesus answered and said to them, "Most assuredly, I say to you, **the Son can do nothing of Himself, but what He sees the Father do;** for whatever He does, the Son also does in like manner. For **the Father** loves the Son, and **shows Him all things that He Himself does;** and He will show Him greater works than these, that you may marvel. For as the Father raises the dead and gives life to them, even so the Son gives life to whom He will. **For the Father judges no one, but has committed all judgment to the Son, that all should honor the Son just as they honor the Father.** He who does not honor the Son does not honor the Father who sent Him." (John 5:19–23, emphasis added)*

VIII. HE WAS CLOTHED WITH A ROBE DIPPED IN BLOOD

A. In Revelation 19, John sees that the One who is revealed in Isaiah 63:1–7 is Jesus Christ of Nazareth, the Son of God.

He Himself treads the winepress of the fierceness and wrath of Almighty God. (Revelation 19:15)

B. The Robe of Jesus has two dimensions.

*For He put on **righteousness as a breastplate,** and a **helmet of salvation** on His head; He put on **the garments of vengeance for clothing,** and **was clad with zeal as a cloak.** According to their deeds, accordingly **He will repay, fury to His adversaries, recompense to His enemies; the coastlands He will fully repay.** (Isaiah 59:17–18, emphasis added)*

1. It is the garment of vengeance (Isaiah 59:17–18).

    a. ***Righteousness***

    b. ***Salvation***

    c. ***Vengeance***

2. It is as the Priestly garments connected with the order of Melchizedek, which are related to the day of His wrath (Psalm 110).

C. I believe that it is significant that the robe that Jesus is wearing is possibly a priestly garment, because I believe that the Armageddon Campaign will be fought by prophetic, intercessory and worship decrees by the Son of God. These decrees will result in the full response of Heaven destroying God's enemies. The battle of 2 Chronicles 20:14–23, I believe, is a prophetic picture of the Armageddon Campaign.

Then the Spirit of the LORD came upon Jahaziel the son of Zechariah, the son of Benaiah, the son of Jeiel, the son of Mattaniah, a Levite of the sons of Asaph, in the midst of the assembly. And he said, "Listen, all you of Judah and you inhabitants of Jerusalem, and you, **King Jehoshaphat!** *Thus says the LORD to you: 'Do not be afraid nor dismayed because of this great multitude,* **for the battle is not yours, but God's.** *Tomorrow go down against them. They will surely come up by the Ascent of Ziz, and you will find them at the end of the brook before the Wilderness of Jeruel.* **You will not need to fight in this battle. Position yourselves, stand still and see the salvation of the LORD, who is with you, O Judah and Jerusalem!'** *Do not fear or be dismayed; tomorrow go out against them, for the LORD is with you." And* **Jehoshaphat** *bowed his head with his face to the ground, and all Judah and the inhabitants of Jerusalem bowed before the LORD, worshiping the LORD. Then the Levites of the children of the Kohathites and of the children of the Korahites stood up to praise the LORD God of Israel with voices loud and high. So they rose early in the morning and went out into the Wilderness of Tekoa; and as they went out,* **Jehoshaphat** *stood and said,* **"Hear me, O Judah and you inhabitants of Jerusalem: Believe in the LORD your God, and you shall be established; believe His prophets, and you shall prosper." And when he had consulted with the people, he appointed those who should sing to the LORD, and who should praise the beauty of holiness, as they went out before the army** *and were saying: "Praise the LORD, for His mercy endures forever." Now when they began to sing and to praise,* **the LORD set ambushes** *against the people of Ammon, Moab, and Mount Seir, who had come against Judah; and* **they were defeated.** *For the people of Ammon and Moab stood up against the inhabitants of Mount Seir to* **utterly kill and destroy them.** *And when they had made an end of the inhabitants of Seir,* **they helped to destroy one another.** *(2 Chronicles 20:14–23, emphasis added)*

And the **armies in heaven, clothed in fine linen, white and clean,** *followed Him on white horses. (Revelation 19:14, emphasis added)*

D.   The armies of Heaven who are following Him will also be clothed in priestly garments, emphasizing their partnership with the Son of God in declaring prophetic, intercessory and worship decrees.

*The L*ORD *said to my Lord, "Sit at My right hand, till I make Your enemies Your footstool"* (Millennial Reign: 1 Corinthians 15:25). *The L*ORD *shall send the **rod of Your strength*** (Revelation 19:15) *out of Zion. Rule in the midst of Your enemies! Your people shall be volunteers in **the day of Your power*** (the battle of Armageddon)*; in the beauties of holiness* (Revelation 19:14)*, **from the womb of the morning*** (Romans 13:12)*, You have the dew of Your youth. The L*ORD *has sworn and will not relent, **"You are a priest forever according to the order of Melchizedek"*** (Revelation 19:13). *The Lord is at Your right hand; He shall execute kings in **the day of His wrath*** (the battle of Armageddon). *He shall judge among the nations, **He shall fill the places with dead bodies*** (Isaiah 66:16), *He shall execute the heads of many countries. He shall drink of the brook by the wayside; therefore He shall lift up the head. (Psalm 110, emphasis and parenthetical comments added)*

Session Sixteen: The Exceeding Greatness of His Power

I. **GRACE: THE POWER THAT SAVES AND THE POWER THAT SUSTAINS**

For the grace of God (the power of God) *that brings salvation has appeared to all men, teaching us that, denying ungodliness and worldly lusts, we should live soberly, righteously, and godly in the present age, looking for the blessed hope and glorious appearing of our great God and Savior Jesus Christ, who gave Himself for us, that He might redeem us from every lawless deed and purify for Himself His own special people, zealous for good works. Speak these things, exhort, and rebuke with all authority. Let no one despise you. (Titus 2:11–15, parenthetical comment added)*

A. Mercy **extends God's forgiveness** and grace **imparts God's enabling power** to our inner man to walk in righteousness and to function in ministry.

B. It is the mercy of God that forgives us of our sin. The grace of God is that which saves us and sustains us in righteousness as we access His grace through our fellowship with the Holy Spirit.

   . . . Through whom also we have access by faith into this grace in which we stand, and rejoice in hope of the glory of God. (Romans 5:2)

C. Grace, in the simplest terms, is the power of God for life and godliness that comes through encountering the knowledge of God. Grace is the life-giving presence, the resurrection power, of God.

   . . . And declared to be the Son of God with power according to the Spirit of holiness, by the resurrection from the dead. (Romans 1:4)

II. **JUSTIFICATION: UNDERSTANDING THE PURPOSE OF THE FREE GIFT OF SALVATION**

A. The mercy and the grace of God came to us for justification, sanctification and glorification.

   1. Justification—acceptance by God.

   2. Sanctification—holiness (being mature in love, pursuing and growing into the fullness of God).

3.   Glorification—entering into our eternal destiny and receiving resurrected bodies.

B.   The purpose of our justification is our sanctification unto our glorification at the Second Coming of Christ when He returns to establish His Kingdom on the earth forever.

C.   If we misunderstand the purpose of justification (God's acceptance and acquittal of our crimes before the court of Heaven), we will then misunderstand the purpose of His grace. He gives mercy to the repentant heart in Christ, that He might give power for life and godliness.

*Therefore, having been **justified by faith,** we have peace with God through our Lord Jesus Christ, **through whom also we have access by faith into this grace** in which we stand, and rejoice in hope of the glory of God. (Romans 5:1–2, emphasis added)*

D.   Before we had salvation we didn't have the strength at all to do right; but now that we have obtained mercy, we can access the strength of God, which is His **grace.**

For when we were still without strength, in due time Christ died for the ungodly. (Romans 5:6)

And you He made alive, who were dead in trespasses and sins, in which you once walked according to the course of this world, according to the prince of the power of the air, the spirit who now works in the sons of disobedience, among whom also we all once conducted ourselves in the lusts of our flesh, fulfilling the desires of the flesh and of the mind, and were by nature children of wrath, just as the others. (Ephesians 2:1–3)

III.   BLESSED WITH EVERY SPIRITUAL BLESSING IN HEAVENLY PLACES IN CHRIST

*Blessed be the God and Father of our Lord Jesus Christ, who has blessed us with every **spiritual blessing** (grace—spiritual pleasures) in the heavenly places in Christ . . . (Ephesians 1:3, emphasis and parenthetical comment added)*

A.   The reality of the born again experience has given us the privilege to experience the wealth of Heaven—grace. By the Spirit who raised us and dwells in us, we are able to access the full presence of God. That is the spiritual blessing, the grace of God. We really have access to every spiritual blessing, the full presence of God and knowledge of Him.

> *. . . And **raised us up together, and made us sit together in the heavenly places** in Christ Jesus . . . (Ephesians 2:6, emphasis added)*

> *To them God willed to make known what are **the riches of the glory of this mystery** among the Gentiles: which is **Christ in you,** the hope of glory. (Colossians 1:27, emphasis added)*

B.   Encountering the grace of God is encountering the superior pleasures of the Gospel of Jesus Christ. There are many Bible verses that call us to experience the pleasures of God's grace.

> *For You will not leave my soul in Sheol, nor will You allow Your Holy One to see corruption. You will show me the path of life; in Your presence is fullness of joy; at Your right hand are pleasures forevermore. (Psalm 16:10–11)*

> *They are abundantly satisfied with the fullness of Your house, and You give them drink from the river of Your pleasures. (Psalm 36:8)*

C.   *If there lurks in most modern minds the notion that to desire our own good and earnestly to hope for the enjoyment of it is a bad thing, I submit that this notion has crept in from Kant and the Stoics and is no part of the Christian faith. Indeed, if we consider the unblushing promises of reward and the staggering nature of the rewards promised in the gospels, it would seem that Our Lord finds our desires, not too strong, but too weak. We are half-hearted creatures, fooling about with drink and sex and ambition when infinite joy is offered us, like an ignorant child who wants to go on making mud pies in a slum because he cannot imagine what is meant by the offer of a holiday at the sea. We are far too easily pleased.*[1]

D.   He chose (justified) us for the purpose of giving access to the grace of God in pursuit of a blameless and holy life in love. He chose us that we might become voluntary lovers and give ourselves to the beauty of holiness.

E.   Holiness is a call to true happiness, freedom, profound pleasure, peace and emotional wholeness, to be free without shame, guilt or accusation.

---

1   Lewis, C.S. *The Weight of Glory.* http://en.wikiquote.org/wiki/C.S._Lewis.

F.   The saints (mystics) of old at times had such powerful encounters with the grace of God that they felt beside themselves in holy ecstasy. Encountering the grace of God leads us to spiritual ecstasy in heavenly places.

IV.   CHOSEN BEFORE THE FOUNDATIONS OF THE WORLD FOR VOLUNTARY LOVE

> *. . . Just as He chose us in Him before the foundation of the world, that we should be holy and without blame before Him in love, having predestined us to adoption as sons by Jesus Christ to Himself, according to the good pleasure of His will, ⁶ to the praise of the glory of His grace, by which He made us accepted in the Beloved. (Ephesians 1:4–6)*

A.   That God chose us in Christ reveals to us the depth of His love for us. While we were in enmity with God, He was rich in mercy and He had deep, fiery, transcendent affections and desires for us. Touching the affections of God through prayer and the Word will awaken our hearts in love unto giving ourselves to Him in greater abandon.

> *In this is love, not that we loved God, but that He loved us and sent His Son to be the propitiation for our sins. (1 John 4:10)*

> *We love Him because He first loved us. (1 John 4:19)*

B.   Before Genesis 1, it was in the eternal counsel of the Godhead to use His Son for our redemption. This eternal plan of redemption is the only plan, and there is no back up plan.

C.   He wants us to become voluntary lovers so we can access the grace of God, which will empower us to attain the highest that God has for us in His grace, leading us into lives of righteousness.

D.   The message of God's grace is not for the strong, but for the weak.

> *For when **we were still without strength,** in due time Christ died for the ungodly. (Romans 5:6, emphasis added)*

> ***Blessed is the man whose strength is in You, whose heart is set on pilgrimage.** As they pass through the Valley of Baca, they make it a spring; the rain also covers it with pools. **They go from strength to strength; each one appears before God** in Zion. (Psalm 84:5–7, emphasis added)*

My grace is sufficient for you, for My **strength** *is made perfect in weakness. (2 Corinthians 12:9, emphasis added)*

E.   One of the purposes of the plan of redemption is to manifest the Lord's leadership and kindness so that forever we would magnify the power of His grace.

. . . Having predestined us to adoption as sons by Jesus Christ to Himself, according to the good pleasure of His will, to the praise of the glory of His grace . . . (Ephesians 1:5–6)

F.   Ephesians 1:5–15 unfolds the mystery of redemption unto the celebration of the true grace of God throughout eternity.

. . . That in the ages to come He might show the exceeding riches of His grace in His kindness toward us in Christ Jesus. For by grace you have been saved through faith, and that not of yourselves; it is the gift of God . . . (Ephesians 2:7–8)

V.   WISDOM AND REVELATION: SEARCHING OUT THE KNOWLDEGE OF HIS GRACE

. . . That the God of our Lord Jesus Christ, the Father of glory, may give to you the spirit of wisdom and revelation in the knowledge of Him, the eyes of your understanding being enlightened; that you may know what is the hope of His calling, what are the riches of the glory of His inheritance in the saints, and what is the exceeding greatness of His power toward us who believe . . . (Ephesians 1:17–19)

A.   The prayer of the Apostle Paul for the church of Ephesus (Ephesians 1:17–19) is a powerful prayer for encountering the knowledge of God. Paul prays this prayer because as we grow in the knowledge of God through study and meditation on the Word of God, we will gain insight into the glorious plan of redemption. The revelation of the personality of God will give us insight into the knowledge of redemption.

B.   We are to be **complete** in our obedience (2 Corinthians 13:9,11; Philippians 1:6; Colossians 4:12; 2 Timothy 3:17; Hebrews 13:20–21; James 1:4); **perfect** (Matthew 5:48,19:21; John 17:23; Galatians 3:3; Ephesians 4:13; Colossians 1:28; 1 Thessalonians 3:10; James 2:22, 3:2; 1 Peter 5:10; Revelation 3:2); **mature** (Philippians 3:15); **blameless** (Luke 1:6; 1 Corinthians 1:6–8; Philippians 2:15; 1 Thessalonians 3:13, 5:23; 1 Timothy 3:2,10, 5:5–7, 6:14; 2 Peter 3:14); **without spot** (Ephesians 5:27).

*Therefore you shall be **perfect** (mature), just as your Father in heaven is perfect. (Matthew 5:48, emphasis and parenthetical comment added)*

*. . . That He might present her to Himself a **glorious church, not having spot** or wrinkle or **any** such thing, but that she should be holy and **without blemish.** (Ephesians 5:27, emphasis added)*

*Now to Him who is able to **keep you from stumbling,** and **to present you faultless** (blameless in character) before the presence of His glory with exceeding joy . . . (Jude 24, emphasis added)*

*But may the God of all grace, who called us to His eternal glory by Christ Jesus, after you have suffered a while, **perfect,** establish, strengthen, and settle you. (1 Peter 5:10, emphasis added)*

C.   There is a fourfold result of encountering the knowledge of God that empowers and energizes the heart, enabling us to respond to deeper levels of righteousness unto our obedience, becoming complete in Christ.

1.   The eyes of our understanding being enlightened—dynamic energizing of the heart through intimacy with the Lord.

2.   The hope of His calling—we get connected with our eternal destiny in God (eschatology), the hope of glory.

3.   The riches of the glory of His inheritance in the saints—what God wants is us. We are His magnificent obsession.

*When I consider Your heavens, the work of Your fingers, the moon and the stars, which You have ordained, **what is man that You are mindful** (with thoughts about humans) **of him,** and the son of man that You visit him? (Psalm 8:3–4, emphasis and parenthetical comment added)*

*Many, O LORD my God, are Your wonderful works which You have done; and **Your thoughts toward us cannot be recounted to You in order;** if I would declare and speak of them, **they are more than can be numbered.** (Psalm 40:5, emphasis added)*

*How **precious also are Your thoughts** to me, O God! **How great is the sum of them!** If I should count them, **they would be more in number than the sand;** when I awake, I am still with You. (Psalm 139:17–18, emphasis added)*

4.   The exceeding greatness of His power toward us who believe— we come to know the fullness of the power in the grace of God that is available to us.

VI.   THE EXCEEDING GREATNESS OF HIS POWER TOWARD US WHO BELIEVE

. . . And what is the exceeding greatness of His power toward us who believe, according to the working of His mighty power which He worked in Christ when He raised Him from the dead and seated Him at His right hand in the heavenly places, far above all principality and power and might and dominion, and every name that is named, not only in this age but also in that which is to come. (Ephesians 1:19–21)

A.   The grace of God is the power of the Resurrection made available to us. We not only have the power of Genesis 1 available to us for our wholeness and sanctification, but the same power that raised Christ from the dead is toward us if we strive through living lives of communion and cooperation with the indwelling Spirit.

B.   The power toward us who believe is according to the power of the Father that worked in Christ, raised Him from the dead and through which He ascended into Heaven. The power of the Resurrection is the Spirit of Holiness.

. . . And declared to be the Son of God with power according to the Spirit of holiness, by the resurrection from the dead. (Romans 1:4)

C.   The power that created the worlds (the power that raised Christ from the dead) is the grace that is available to help us change our appetites and overcome sin, the lust of the flesh, the lust of the eye and the boastful pride of life.

But if the Spirit of Him who raised Jesus from the dead dwells in you, He who raised Christ from the dead will also give life to your mortal bodies through His Spirit who dwells in you. (Romans 8:11)

D.   By grace we were brought to newness of life. We were dead, not being able to respond to God, but being rich in mercy, He forgave those who repented before Him and by grace made us alive in Christ.

E.   Grace is the power of Genesis 1 and the power of the Resurrection! By it we've been delivered from the kingdom of darkness and conveyed into the kingdom of the Son of His love. He has established us by His power.

Have you not known? Have you not heard? The everlasting God, the Lord, the Creator of the ends of the earth, neither faints nor is weary. His understanding is unsearchable. He gives power to the weak, and to those who have no might He increases strength. Even the youths shall faint and be weary, and the young men shall utterly fall, but those who wait on the Lord shall renew their strength; they shall mount up with wings like eagles, they shall run and not be weary, they shall walk and not faint. (Isaiah 40:28–31)

VII.   WITH DIFFICULTY THE RIGHTEOUS ARE SAVED

For it is time for judgment to begin with the household of God; and if it begins with us first, what will be the outcome for those who do not obey the gospel of God? ***And if it is with difficulty that the righteous is saved,*** *what will become of the godless man and the sinner?* (*1 Peter 4:17–18 NASB, emphasis added*)

A.   The question is that if the power of Genesis 1 and the power of the Resurrection are available to us, then why is it so difficult for us to find freedom? The answer is that there are pockets of resistance and areas of unperceived agreement with darkness. These must be brought under the leadership of Jesus Christ. **He chose us in Christ that we might become voluntary lovers. We must by the act of our own free will do our part and God will do His. He will not violate our free will.**

   Behold, You desire truth in the inward parts, and in the hidden part You will make me to know wisdom. (Psalm 51:6)

B.   We are to strive to live in full obedience and to experience the Spirit's life. **We do not strive to earn forgiveness,** but to live in holiness, that is, to receive a breakthrough in the heart, experiencing the pleasures of grace forevermore (loving what God loves).

   *Because **narrow** is the gate and **difficult is the way** which leads to life (experiencing life in the inner man), and there are **few** who find it. (Matthew 7:14, emphasis and parenthetical comment added)*

C.   We strive, or exert exceptional care and energy, to bring ourselves before the fire of God's grace so as to receive freely from His fire at the heart level. This is called spiritual violence, or pressing in for the prize, "cutting off our right hand" or "plucking out our eye" (Matthew 5:29–30). This striving involves our time, energy, money and thinking.

D.   As we give ourselves to communing with the Holy Spirit, we then go from strength to strength, glory to glory, and receive grace for grace.

*They go from **strength to strength;** each one appears before God in Zion. (Psalm 84:7, emphasis added)*

*But we all, with unveiled face, beholding as in a mirror the glory of the Lord, are being transformed into the same image from **glory to glory,** just as by the Spirit of the Lord. (2 Corinthians 3:18, emphasis added)*

*And of His fullness we have all received, and **grace for grace.** (John 1:16, emphasis added)*

E.   We access the grace of God by talking to the Holy Spirit who lives inside of us. We give ourselves to study and meditation on the Word and fasting. **We don't earn the grace of God, but these intensify our posture of receptivity before Him.**

F.   **Principle: We walk in the grace of God by talking with the Spirit.** The fundamental and introductory way to **walk in the Spirit** is by maintaining an active dialogue with the indwelling Spirit. This is key to our transformation and renewal. **Start by talking directly to the Spirit five to ten times a day for three to five minutes at a time.** We must renounce all that minimizes the Holy Spirit's work in our hearts. We can grow in our experience of the indwelling Holy Spirit.

VIII.   PRACTICAL EXAMPLES

A.   **Thank you**—we recognize the Spirit's presence in us simply by thanking Him for it and then by giving ourselves to Him. We pray, "Thank you, Holy Spirit, for Your bright presence in me; I am fully Yours and You are mine; now manifest Yourself to me."

I am my Beloved's, and my Beloved is mine. (Song 6:3)

*He who has My commandments and **keeps** them, it is he who loves Me . . . I will love him and **manifest** Myself to him. (John 14:21, emphasis added)*

B.   **Teach me**—we ask Him to lead us into truth, praying, "Consuming Fire, teach me Your ways."

*. . . The Holy Spirit . . . will **teach you all things** . . . (John 14:26, emphasis added)*

*. . . The Spirit of truth . . . will **guide you into all truth** . . . He will tell you **things to come.** (John 16:13, emphasis added)*

. . . May give to you the spirit of wisdom and revelation in the knowledge of Him . . . (Ephesians 1:17)

C.   **Lead me**—we thank the indwelling Spirit for His leadership inside of us. We pray, "Holy Spirit, lead me in my speech (Psalm 141:3), into divine appointments and opportunities (Romans 8:14) and away from Satan's traps and temptations (Matthew 6:13). I love Your leadership; I need Your leadership."

*Set a **guard,** O LORD, over my mouth; **keep watch** over the door of my lips. (Psalm 141:3, emphasis added)*

*For as many as are **led by the Spirit of God,** these are sons of God. (Romans 8:14, emphasis added)*

And do not lead us into temptation (lead me from it)*, but deliver us from the evil one. (Matthew 6:13, parenthetical comment added)*

D.   **Strengthen me**—we thank Him for the strength that is already in us by His indwelling Presence (Galatians 5:22–23). We pray, "O Living Flame of Love, thank you for the presence of Your indestructible love, peace, patience and self-control. Thank you for Your commitment to war against my flesh and to release the fear of God into my heart."
       *. . . To be **strengthened** with might through **His Spirit in the inner man** . . . (Ephesians 3:16, emphasis added)*

For the flesh lusts (wars) *against the Spirit, and the **Spirit against the flesh** . . . But the fruit of the Spirit is love, joy, peace, longsuffering, kindness, goodness, faithfulness, gentleness, self-control. (Galatians 5:17, 22–23, emphasis and parenthetical comment added)*

Unite my heart to fear *Your name. (Psalm 86:11, emphasis added)*

Session Seventeen: The Knowledge of God—Pursuing God's Holy Heart

I. **THE DEEP THINGS OF GOD**

   A. The reality of God's emotions is not just an issue of attributing human characteristics and behaviors to God as though His emotions are human. His emotions are divine and are transcendent in nature. They are spiritual and divine in origin, not earthly and soulish.

   B. God's emotions are experienced in the context of embracing the life of the Cross.

   But now your kingdom shall not continue. ***The L*ord *has sought for Himself a man after His own heart*** *and the L*ord *has commanded him to be commander over His people, because you have not kept what the L*ord *commanded you. (1 Samuel 13:14, emphasis added)*

   And when He had removed him, He raised up for them David as king, to whom also He gave testimony and said, "I have found David the son of Jesse, ***a man after My own heart, who will do all My will.*** *" (Acts 13:22, emphasis added)*

   If anyone desires to ***come after Me, let him deny himself, and take up his cross,*** *and follow Me. For whoever desires to save his life will lose it, but whoever loses his life for My sake will find it. (Matthew 16:24–25, emphasis added)*

   C. All of God's emotions are deep and transcendent expressions of His divine being and essence—for example: love, wrath, jealousy, joy, delight and pleasure. The emotions of God are not soulish, but spiritual, though they can be powerfully experienced in the soul of the born again believer.

   D. I believe that experiencing the conviction of the Spirit is an encounter with the emotions of God. Conviction allows us to experience God's zeal for righteousness and His hatred toward wickedness.

   "For ***My thoughts are not your thoughts,*** *nor are your ways My ways," says the L*ord*. "For as the heavens are higher than the earth, so are* ***My ways higher than your ways, and My thoughts than your thoughts.*** *" (Isaiah 55:8–9, emphasis added)*

II.   THE CROSS: THE BEGINNING POINT OF THE EMOTIONS OF GOD

A.   The Cross is the beginning point for pursuing God's emotions. The revelation of true love and affection is revealed in the realm of the Cross.

B.   Without the revelation of the Cross, we see the reality of God's emotions through the filter of our own sensuality and media with entertainment-toxified souls, thus making the Bridal Paradigm sensual.

C.   The Bridal Paradigm and the revelation of the Bridegroom God are to awaken holy, pure, righteous and fiery affections in our hearts for God and His Christ.

*Who is wise and understanding among you? Let him show by good conduct that his works are done in the meekness of wisdom. But if you have **bitter envy and self-seeking** in your hearts, do not boast and lie against the truth. **This wisdom** does not descend from above, but **is earthly, sensual, demonic.** For where envy and self-seeking exist, confusion and every evil thing are there. (James 3:13–16, emphasis added)*

D.   Anything that is experienced outside the life of the Cross is a self-seeking surge that looks to be satisfied by the lifting of our souls to another and the worship of a God created in our own image. As a result, we are tempted to relate to God on the same basis, as though His emotions are like ours.

E.   Being sensual in this context refers to our own preoccupation with earthbound realities that are secondary, some legitimate and some illegitimate, to satisfy our appetites.

F.   The Cross of Christ gives us profound insight into the deep things of God in that the Cross is at the very center of who God is.

III.   AFTER GOD'S OWN HEART

A.   Being a man after God's own heart is what set David apart from all other men and women in the Word of God. There were others who lived extraordinary lives before God in obedience—like Daniel, Job, Moses, Joseph, Esther and Deborah, to mention a few—but David had a unique standing before God.

B.   David's own accomplishments, though many and powerful, were not the things that caused him to be recognized in a unique way throughout the corridors of history.

> *But now your kingdom shall not continue.* ***The Lord has sought for Himself a man after His own heart,*** *and the Lord has commanded him to be commander over His people, because you have not kept what the Lord commanded you. (1 Samuel 13:14, emphasis added)*

> *And when He had removed him, He raised up for them David as king, to whom also He gave testimony and said, "I have found David the son of Jesse,* ***a man after My own heart, who will do all My will."*** *(Acts 13:22, emphasis added)*

C.   A man or woman after God's heart refers to a person whose single focus, passion and vision is to pursue and understand His emotions. God is not a stale stoic. He is the author of the realm of emotions because He possesses powerful transcendent emotions within Himself.

D.   A people after God's own heart are a people who pursue and encounter the emotions of God that fuel abandonment in their spirit and soul.

E.   When we encounter the knowledge of God and the power of His emotions toward us in our being (Colossians 1:27), it will produce a heart that is ablaze in love.

> *And I have declared to them* ***Your name,*** *and will declare it, that* ***the love with which You loved Me may be in them,*** *and I in them. (John 17:26, emphasis added)*

> *In this is love,* ***not that we loved God, but that He loved us*** *and sent His Son to be the propitiation for our sins. (1 John 4:10, emphasis added)*

> *We love Him because He first loved us. (1 John 4:19)*

IV.   BECOMING A PERSON AFTER GOD'S OWN HEART

A.   It's vital that we become **students of God's emotions.** The revelation of the heart of God is what will equip us to become lovesick worshipers. The longer we sit before the fire of God's emotions to encounter them and to gaze upon them, the more our hearts will be equipped in love, righteousness and holiness.

B. We want to be filled with the knowledge of His will, or the revelation of the longings of His transcendence, and then grow in wisdom and spiritual understanding of His heart. Encountering of the knowledge of God will cause us to walk worthy, equipped to live lives pleasing to Him and Him alone.

C. **Becoming a person after God's own heart also means that we have a strong vision and commitment to live lives of 100 percent obedience.** This commitment does not mean that we attain to it, but that we pursue it with all of our being in the grace of God.

D. David was a man who had a cry in his heart to belong to the Lord, even though he made many mistakes and sometimes committed horrendous sins that cost the lives of many. Our sincere intentions to obey God are very significant and powerful before Him. Our hearts' sincere but weak cry to be His is powerful in the heart of God.

Not that I have already attained, or am already perfected (mature)*; but I press on, that I may lay hold of that for which Christ Jesus has also laid hold of me. Brethren,* **I do not count myself to have apprehended** (attained 100 percent obedience and maturity)*; but one thing I do, forgetting those things which are behind and reaching forward to those things which are ahead, I press toward the goal for the prize of the upward call of God in Christ Jesus. (Philippians 3:12–14, emphasis and parenthetical comments added)*

Then He spoke many things to them in parables, saying: "Behold, a sower went out to sow. And as he sowed, some seed fell by the wayside; and the birds came and devoured them. Some fell on stony places, where they did not have much earth; and they immediately sprang up because they had no depth of earth. But when the sun was up they were scorched, and because they had no root they withered away. And some fell among thorns, and the thorns sprang up and choked them. **But others fell on good ground and yielded a crop: some a hundredfold, some sixty, some thirty. He who has ears to hear, let him hear!"** *(Matthew 13:3–9, emphasis added)*

E. To be after God's own heart means that we contend for the fullness of the purpose of God in a generation. David did all the will of God in his generation. As we draw nearer to the Lord's return, we want to give ourselves to partnering with Him concerning the things that are on His heart in this crucial hour of human history (see the books of Revelation and Daniel).

V. THE EMOTIONS OF GOD

A. David was a man who encountered the power of God's emotional make up. The Psalms are filled with insight into David's heart-journey after the heart of God.

B. In Psalm 36:8, David describes the heart of God as a rushing river of pleasure and delight by which we can be abundantly satisfied. Psalm 42:7 describes the heart of God as a mighty rushing waterfall that flows from the very depths of God's being.

C. Having our being filled with the knowledge of God is what will produce unwavering maturity in our lives. It is the fastest and most sure road to spiritual maturity.

> *And He Himself gave some to be apostles, some prophets, some evangelists, and some pastors and teachers, for the **equipping of the saints** for the work of ministry, for **the edifying** of the body of Christ, till we all come **to the unity of the faith and of the knowledge of the Son of God, to a perfect man** (mature), to the measure of the stature of the fullness of Christ; that we should **no longer be children, tossed to and fro and carried about with every wind of doctrine,** by the trickery of men, in the cunning craftiness of deceitful plotting, but, speaking the truth in love, **may grow up in all things into Him who is the head— Christ**—from whom the whole body, joined and knit together by what every joint supplies, according to the effective working by which every part does its share, **causes growth of the body for the edifying of itself in love.** (Ephesians 4:11–16, emphasis and parenthetical comment added)*

VI. GOD ENJOYS US IN OUR WEAKNESS

A. The three things that powerfully transformed my life as it relates to my interaction with God are, first, the knowledge of Christ's sympathy toward me in weakness and temptation (**Hebrews 4:14–16**). Second, the powerful, transforming truth that God enjoys me in my weakness (**Song of Solomon 1:5**). Third, the reality that God is profoundly affected by me in His being (**Song of Solomon 4:9**).

> *Seeing then that we have a great High Priest who has passed through the heavens, Jesus the Son of God, let us hold fast our confession. **For we do not have a High Priest who cannot sympathize with our weaknesses,** but was in all points tempted as we are, yet without sin. **Let us therefore come boldly to the throne of grace,** that we may obtain mercy and find grace to help in time of need. (Hebrews 4:14–16, emphasis added)*

I am dark, but lovely, O daughters of Jerusalem, like the tents of Kedar, like the curtains of Solomon. (Song of Solomon 1:5, emphasis added)

As the Father loved Me, I also have loved you; abide in My love. (John 15:9, emphasis added)

B.   Something powerful happens in our spirits every time the Lord tells us how He feels about us. It truly calms and quiets our souls, and righteousness begins to seem wise and within our reach in the grace of God. Many believers are disconnected from that reality.

C.   One of the most powerful realities is that we have a God who is not apathetic. We serve a God who we not only experience, but who experiences us.

*You have **ravished** My heart, My sister, My spouse; you have **ravished** My heart with **one look of your eyes,** with one link of your necklace. (Song of Solomon 4:9, emphasis added)*

D.   To ravish means: to seize and **take away by violence;** to overcome with emotion (as joy or delight).[1]

*And from the days of John the Baptist until now **the kingdom of heaven suffers violence,** and the violent take it by force. (Matthew 11:12, emphasis added)*

*Turn **your eyes** away from Me, for **they have overcome Me.** Your hair is like a flock of goats going down from Gilead. (Song of Solomon 6:5, emphasis added)*

*For as a young man marries a virgin, so shall your sons marry you; and **as the bridegroom rejoices over the bride, so shall your God rejoice over you.** (Isaiah 62:5, emphasis added)*

The LORD *your God in your midst, the Mighty One, will save; He will rejoice over you with gladness, He will quiet you with His love, **He will rejoice over you with singing.** (Zephaniah 3:17, emphasis added)*

E.   We do not just experience God. God experiences us—the weak yet deepest reaches of our hearts in Christ Jesus affect that heart of God, and He moves toward us accordingly.

Draw near to God and He will draw near to you. (James 4:8)

---

1   "Ravish." Dictionary.com. *Dictionary.com Unabridged (v 1.1).* Random House, Inc. http://dictionary.reference.com/browse/ravish. Accessed January 10, 2008.

F.   Our wrong views of God will lead to some of the greatest regrets when we stand before the judgment seat of Christ and we see how exquisite, lovely and beautiful He is. The enemy seeks to destroy and skew the revelation of the knowledge of God in our minds and hearts.

> *However, we speak wisdom among those who are mature, yet not the wisdom of this age, nor of the rulers of this age, who are coming to nothing. But we speak the wisdom of God in a mystery, **the hidden wisdom which God ordained before the ages for our glory,** which none of the rulers of this age knew; for had they known, they would not have crucified the Lord of glory But as it is written: "Eye has not seen, nor ear heard, nor have entered into the heart of man the things which God has prepared for those who love Him." **But God has revealed them to us through His Spirit. For the Spirit searches all things, yes, the deep things of God.** (1 Corinthians 2:6–10, emphasis added)*

VII.   FROM RELIGIOUS SACRIFICE TO HOLY OBSESSION

A.   The Lord is going to release a new approach to holiness in this generation. It will not be new to the Bible, but it will be new to this generation because the Lord is going to reveal the true heart and fuel behind holiness, which is fascination with His glory and beauty.

> *Yet indeed I also **count all things loss for the excellence of the knowledge of Christ** Jesus my Lord, for whom I have suffered the loss of all things, and count them as rubbish, that I may gain Christ . . . (Philippians 3:8, emphasis added)*

> *One thing I have desired of the LORD, that will I seek: That I may dwell in the house of the LORD all the days of my life, **to behold the beauty of the LORD,** and to inquire in His temple. (Psalm 27:4, emphasis added)*

B.   Encountering the delightfulness of the Lord through the Word of God is what will fuel our hearts with love and righteousness. Another definition of holiness could be passion for Jesus or love for God.

VIII.   SECONDARY MOTIVATING FORCES

A.   There are primary and secondary motivating forces that propel us to holiness. Both realities are very powerful, though we are more familiar with the secondary ones.

B.   One of the most common motivating factors to holiness has been within the category of consequences for not doing certain things before the Lord. Some of these consequences have been the fear of shame and humiliation as well as the loss of reward or even the lack of fire.

C.   These are all powerful and true according to the Word of God, but they are secondary to what is in God's heart in relation to how He has designed us and what He wants from us.

IX.   GOD WANTS TO BE UNITED WITH HIS PEOPLE

A.   We were created for love. The primary paradigm of the kingdom at the end of the age will be the Bridal Paradigm. This profound biblical truth has been declared throughout history in segments but will be released in full at the end of the age.

*And **the Spirit and the bride** say, "Come!" And let him who hears say, "Come!" And let him who thirsts come. Whoever desires, let him take the water of life freely. (Revelation 22:17, emphasis added)*

***Then** (at the end of the age) **the kingdom of heaven shall be likened** to ten virgins who took their lamps and went out to meet the bridegroom. (Matthew 25:1, emphasis and parenthetical comment added)*

*"And it shall be, **in that day,**" says the Lord, "that **you will call Me 'My Husband,'** and no longer call Me 'My Master . . .'" (Hosea 2:16, emphasis added)*

B.   God created us for intimacy with Him. The Father's plan and desire is to have a corporate people out of the nations of the earth as the Bride of His Son. This means that God's desire is to have a people who live in His loving embrace forever as God lives in the embrace of God. This embrace is called **abiding.**

*As the Father loved Me, I also have loved you; **abide in My love.** If you keep My commandments, **you will abide in My love,** just as I have kept My Father's commandments and **abide in His love.** (John 15:9–10, emphasis added)*

*"Return, O backsliding children," says the Lord; "for **I am married to you.** I will take you, one from a city and two from a family, and I will bring you to Zion." (Jeremiah 3:14, emphasis added)*

C.   God desires us, and He knows our frame. He knows exactly the best "octane level of fuel" to release into our hearts for the best, most efficient performance of the human engine called the human heart or soul.

D.   The revelation of God's desire to marry His people will ignite our hearts with passion.

*Father, **I desire that they also whom You gave Me may be with Me where I am,** that they may behold My glory which You have given Me; for You loved Me before the foundation of the world. (John 17:24, emphasis added)*

E.   One of the realities revealing God's desire to be united to His people is the truth of His Spirit abiding in us in full. God lives in His people now for union.

To them God willed to make known what are the riches of the glory of this mystery among the Gentiles: which is Christ in you, the hope of glory. *(Colossians 1:27, emphasis added)*

*But he who is joined to the Lord is **one spirit with Him.** (1 Corinthians 6:17, emphasis added)*

F.   The beauty of Jesus is the Father's secret weapon at the end of the age to motivate His people to holiness. We want to get lost in the beauty of the Bridegroom, King and Judge.

In that day the Branch of the Lord shall be beautiful and glorious; *and the fruit of the earth shall be excellent and appealing for those of Israel who have escaped. (Isaiah 4:2, emphasis added)*

G.   The knowledge of God is the central issue for discovering the reality of who God is and who we are. Our identity is found in Christ. Deep things are hidden in the personality of God that are meant for our exhilaration and that will lead to holy abandonment and love.

*Set your mind on things above, not on things on the earth. For you died, and **your life is hidden with Christ in God.** When Christ who is our life appears, then you also will appear with Him in glory. (Colossians 3:2–4, emphasis added)*

*But we speak the wisdom of God in a mystery, **the hidden wisdom** which God **ordained** before the ages for our **glory** (a state of great gratification) . . . (1 Corinthians 2:9, emphasis and parenthetical comment added)*

X.   **BRIDEGROOM FOUNDATIONS**

A.   The God of tenderness—He is quick to forgive.

Thus says the LORD: "Let not the wise man glory in his wisdom, let not the mighty man glory in his might, nor let the rich man glory in his riches; but let him who glories glory in this, that he understands and knows Me, that I am the LORD, exercising lovingkindness, judgment, and righteousness in the earth. For in these I delight," says the LORD. (Jeremiah 9:23–24)

B.   The God of gladness—God is not mostly sad; His gladness is infinite.

C.   The God of burning desire.

D.   The God of jealous anger—Exodus 33:14.

E.   The God of fascinating beauty—Revelation 4–5.

XI.   **THE GAZE THAT STUNS THE HEART**

A.   David, as a shepherd boy, set his heart to be faithful to encounter the Lord in the routines of his vocation. David did not have a very glamorous job. He sat long hours, watching sheep while they grazed in the pastures. Being a shepherd was not considered a very glamorous job at that time. David was babysitting animals for his family chores.

B.   I believe that it was during this time that David decided to cease striving and lay hold of the simplicity of his job and the fact that there were not many distractions. When we are alone and bored, then we run into ourselves and have the greatest opportunity to run into God. I believe that it is during those times that God comes to wrestle with us if we lay hold of that for which we were laid hold of.

*Then Jacob was **left alone;** and a Man wrestled with him until the breaking of day. (Genesis 32:24, emphasis added)*

*Not that I have already attained, or am already perfected; but I press on, that **I may lay hold of that for which Christ Jesus has also laid hold of me.** (Philippians 3:12, emphasis added)*

C.   It was during David's shepherding days that the Lord spoke to Samuel and referred to David as a man after His heart. David, while he was in the pastures doing a mundane job, gave himself to pursuing the heart of God. God responded to the reaches of David's heart with stunning revelation.

But now your kingdom shall not continue. The Lord has sought for Himself **a man after His own heart,** *and the Lord has commanded him to be commander over His people, because you have not kept what the Lord commanded you. (1 Samuel 13:14, emphasis added)*

And when He had removed him (King Saul), *He raised up for them David as king, to whom also He gave testimony and said, "I have found David the son of Jesse, a* **man after My own heart, who will do all My will."** *(Acts 13:22, emphasis and parenthetical comment added)*

XII.   BEHOLDING AND BECOMING

A.   Being a person after God's heart means three things:

1.   We must become students of the emotions of God.

2.   We must pursue (which is different from attaining) 100 percent obedience.

3.   We must contend for the fullness of God's purpose in our lives and generation.

B.   The journey that leads to the transformation of the heart is the beholding and becoming principle. This is the idea that we become what we look at. Our transformation happens within the context of gazing into the heart of God.

But we all, with unveiled face, **beholding as in a mirror the glory of the Lord,** *are being* **transformed into the same image** *from glory to glory, just as by the Spirit of the Lord. (2 Corinthians 3:18, emphasis added)*

C.   Whatever we understand about God's heart toward us is what we become in our hearts toward God. The knowledge of God is absolutely essential. Our inward renewal is in accordance with the knowledge of God. David understood this principle through his desire to behold the beauty of the Lord for all his days (Psalm 27:4).

*. . . And have put on the **new man who is renewed in knowledge according to the image of Him** who created him . . . (Colossians 3:10, emphasis added)*

D.   Encountering God's burning heart is the key to igniting ours. We want to press in by studying and reflecting on the heart of God.

XIII. BEHOLDING THE GLORY OF GOD'S EMOTIONS

A.   At the very core of Paul's theology is the reality of the dim beholding of the glory of God. At the apex of God's glory is the **heart of God or the emotions of God.** Paul, in 1 Corinthians 2:10, calls it the deep things of God. When the Bible speaks of the depths of God, I believe that it is referring to the thunderous depth of His heart.

B.   In the very depths of the **heart of God** are riches, mysteries, wealth and treasures that our hearts have been destined to encounter since before the foundations of the earth.

*But we speak the wisdom of God in **a mystery, the hidden wisdom which God ordained before the ages for our glory,** which none of the rulers of this age knew; for had they known, they would not have crucified the Lord of glory. But as it is written: "Eye has not seen, nor ear heard, nor have entered into the heart of man the things which God has prepared for those who love Him." But God has revealed them to us through His Spirit. **For the Spirit searches all things, yes, the deep things of God.** (1 Corinthians 2:7–10, emphasis added)*

*. . . That their hearts may be encouraged, being knit together in love, **and attaining to all riches of the full assurance of understanding, to the knowledge of the mystery of God,** both of the Father and of Christ, **in whom are hidden all the treasures of wisdom and knowledge.** (Colossians 2:2–3, emphasis added)*

C.   When we encounter or behold God's emotions, there are corresponding emotions that are awakened in us toward Him. We burn for God in as much as we understand that He longs for us first and we taste of that reality. We begin to enjoy God when we understand how much God enjoys us. The most important opinion in our lives is God's opinion and His affection toward us.

XIV.   THE DIVINE PARTNERSHIP

A.   In the journey of transformation, we must understand that there is a dance between us and God. God has a role and we have role. Understanding this is important because our transformation will not happen unless we do our part because God will not do it for us.

B.   We must actively draw near to God, and He will in turn draw to us. We draw near to God through fasting, praying and filling our minds with the Word of God. The journey of repentance starts with changing our way of thinking in particular as it relates to our ideas about God. When we turn to God, He promises to ignite our spirits with the power of His presence.

C.   Beholding God's emotions is something only you can do in your own secret life in God. The truths of His heart must get into the particular language of your heart. No other person can do it for you, and God Himself will not do it for you. We must saturate our thoughts with God's emotions and His passions for us.

D.   The Word of God is our onramp into His heart. It is what I call the transcript of the heart of God. As we read, pray, sing and study the Word of God, it will begin to re-write the code of our hearts. This exercise will lead us to where the words describing God's heart in the Word of God become a part of our heart-language.

*Then Jesus said to those Jews who believed Him, "If you **abide** in My word, you are My disciples indeed. **And you shall know the truth, and the truth shall make you free.**" (John 8:31–32, emphasis added)*

*And do not be conformed to this world, but **be transformed by the renewing of your mind,** that you may prove what is that good and acceptable and perfect will of God. (Romans 12:2, emphasis added)*

E.   The primary way that our minds are renewed is by filling them with the Word of God while we stay away from bad things. Like the farmer, we are to put fertilizer in the soil, sow the seed and pull the weeds, but pulling the weeds alone will not do the job.

XV. TRANSFORMED EMOTIONS AND OBEDIENCE

A. Meditation is key in the process of transformation. In meditation, we speak back to God what we are reading in his Word. Over time, we will begin to feel the impact of it in our souls. It is important that we talk to God about how He thinks and feels about us. The Word of God is alive and powerful, and when we speak back to Him what He thinks it begins to wash our souls.

*For **the word of God is living and powerful,** and sharper than any two-edged sword, piercing even to the division of soul and spirit, and of joints and marrow, and is a **discerner of the thoughts and intents of the heart.** (Hebrews 4:12, emphasis added)*

B. It is important that we give ourselves to long and loving meditation on the Word of God.

C. The transformation of our emotions makes obedience easier and seen as wise and reasonable before God.

D. The reality of beholding the heart of God is practical and essential for every born-again believer for every manner of social status or job description in life.

E. The transformation happens slowly overtime like a seed that is sown into the ground. We must slow our lives down enough to sow and invest in this reality.

F. Four key components:

1. A spirit of obedience.

2. Faith in God's love (testimony about the breakthrough of the love of God upon the heart).

3. A spirit of servanthood.

4. A spirit of devotion.